The Ten Commandments

Of

VBA

For

Microsoft Access Newbies

The Ten Commandments Of VBA

For Microsoft Access Newbies

Practices that produce safe, understandable, and reliable software

Peter N Roth, MSE

TCastle, An imprint of
Engineering Objects International

Contents at a Glance

Contents

Figures

Listings

The Greatest Commandment

You must love the Lord your God with all your heart, with all your soul, and with all your mind. This is the greatest and first commandment. The second resembles it: You must love your neighbor as yourself. On these two commandments hang the whole Law, and the Prophets also.

– Matthew 22:37-40

Dedication

For Mary Jane, Gabrielle, & Rebecca

Acknowledgements

Thanks to Dr Patrick DiVietri, without whose stimulus this book would not exist.

Thanks to Cindy Nichols, Terri Kelly, and Leah Ann Furr for the fun we had with The Inherited Database and The Chicken.

Thanks to .theDBguy, Albert D. Kallal, AllTheGoodNamesWereTaken, Bill Mosca, Daniel Pineault, Dirk Goldgar, Duane Hookom, Gina Whipp, Hans Vogelaar, Ken Sheridan, Scott Diamond, Tom van Stiphout, and all the other denizens of the online Microsoft Access Developers forum. I've been reading your posts for several years. You've been a great help!

Thanks to Jim Muller and Jean Ellis for reading through my attempts at English prose.

Preface

You're an Access Newbie, and find yourself in one or more of the following situations:

- The previous owner of the database that's running the place moved on, and you've inherited it

- You don't have a database, but the boss says, "We need a database! Here's a book and the software! Get crackin'!"

- Your Excel "solution" just doesn't cut it anymore.

- In my case, Cindy said, "Say, Pete - you know something about databases … ?"

Well! You have some learning ahead of you!

The most efficient learning is to focus on the things you need, and avoid the rest. This book therefore presents proven techniques that give you what you need to succeed with VBA, the Microsoft Office programming language. At the same time, the techniques keep you safe and allow you to grow in confidence in your abilities to manage your Access database.

Our assumptions, as we start:

1. Your inherited database may have been designed by another newbie, so it probably has a few quirks.

2. You have a book or two about Microsoft Access besides this one. If not, get some. Check the Bibliography.

3. You may have a little familiarity with VBA, and some familiarity with the VBE (Visual Basic Environment).

4. You may be wondering how to control what you're doing.

5. You know what a *variable*, an *expression*, and a *statement* are; if you are in doubt, check out the VBE Glossary in the VBA help file. And, so you don't have to skip over it at the beginning of this book, go to Appendix A – VBA from Zero for a bit more grounding in the language. It shows the limited set of VBA language constructs you need; elaborating on the limited set is completely unnecessary, so the amount you have to learn is smaller than you think. You might even think of it as learning to speak pidgin VBA.

6. You might be thinking Access is a super-charged spreadsheet. **It's Not**. It's based on the mathematical theory of Dr. Edgar Frank Codd. Search the internet for "Codd's 12 rules".

We developed this text using Access 2010. We tried Access 2016, but found its appearance "lacking". At last, we moved to Microsoft Office 2019. Everything should work in 2010 and later.

Why Microsoft Access?

Access is a one-stop app to build and maintain databases. It supports fast development of

- Tables

- Queries

- Forms

- Reports

- Macros

by newbies, all under one roof. That roof is the Windows desktop; Access has not been ported to Apple computers, nor has the user interface been ported to the internet. Access runs just fine on local and networked systems.

There are many sources that will teach you about all of these. The first commandment "Thou Shalt Get Thee Help" will head you in their direction.

It is enough to say that the material available on VBA is vast, when you consider that not only books are involved, but videos and websites devoted to solving problems. This book's focus is on the macro language "Visual Basic for Applications," hereafter, VBA.

Why VBA?

There are four languages available in Access databases: SQL, with which we write queries; VBA, in which we control the program; and two other macro languages.

- Whereas the two other macro languages allow canned procedures only, VBA is wide open.

- VBA is a powerful language in that you can do almost anything to a Windows computer with it.

- Even so, the language doesn't prevent errors.

What *IS* VBA?

VBA started out as BASIC, the Model T Ford of programming languages. Microsoft remodeled the language into a 1985 Ford Thunderbird. If that comparison is lost on you, let it be noted that VBA is a rounder, smoother, much more powerful language than BASIC, but its roots in the older versions are still visible.

Or, rather, invisible, as there's hardly any built-in safety equipment. We'll fix that here.

On the systems I grew up on, we had to develop ways to protect ourselves. We still need those ways when developing Microsoft Access database code.

VBA is the macro language common to all programs in Microsoft Office, so users of other programs in the Microsoft Office suite may find this book useful too.

Written VBA is called code, but it's designed to be a lot like English. The Visual Basic Environment

(VBE), in which we develop our VBA code, is integrated with, yet hides, an extremely talented and complicated program called the VBA *compiler*, which translates VBA code into instructions digestible by the chips in our computers. The compiler is extremely reliable. When you run across a "compile error" in your code, it doesn't mean that the compiler is in error. It means your code doesn't play by the compiler's rules.

Because of the extraordinary integration of all of the parts of Access, we may have to present some topics with a little hand-waving. Bear with us. Details will follow.

The organization of VBA for Microsoft Access (and all of Microsoft Office) is like *Matryoshka*, or Russian Nesting dolls.

The outer layer is the VBE, separate from (but tightly integrated with) the database environment in which we build Tables, Queries, Forms and Reports.

The VBE contains three Module containers:

1. Microsoft Access Class Objects

2. Modules

3. Class Modules

Each container may contain manifold Modules. The Public contents of each Module may rely on the Public contents of the other Modules, and any References you supply.

Each Module contains VBA code, organized as:

- Declarations
- Procedures

Declarations inform the VBA compiler of the data types we specify for our calculations.

Procedures are program units that contain Declarations, Constructs, and Statements that combine to perform a calculation.

- Constructs are formal Statements that control the flow of a calculation.

- Statements perform the calculation, and call on other procedures to contribute to the effort.

At this point, we're at the VBA code level, the innermost Matryoshka doll, and this is as far as we need to go.

Commandments?

We might look at commandments as a set of rules designed to limit our freedom. That's true. But when freedom is *un*limited, there is a possibility that freedom becomes license. On the other hand, if commandments are instructions that tell how a thing is *supposed* to function, amplifying safety, reliability, and efficiency, then it is worth looking at what they have to say, and then obeying them.

Peter N Roth
January 2020

Introduction

For comfort's sake, we need to set up two environments: The Access database environment, and the VBA environment. Then we need to consider our audience.

Setup

Adjust the Quick Access Toolbar (QAT)

Put some buttons on the QAT. Access assigns a number to each of these QAT buttons, which will allow you to select things by pressing Alt+number. The buttons to add:

1. Datasheet view

2. Design View

3. Form View

4. Layout View

5. Print Preview

6. SQL View

7. Clear Grid

Go to the Access Options menu. In Access 2010, that's File | Options | Quick Access Toolbar. In the "Choose commands from" dropdown, select "All Commands". Select in the left column of the dialog, 'Datasheet View'. Click the 'Add' button to add Datasheet View to the QAT. In turn, do the same with each of the following: 'Design View', 'Form View', 'Layout view', 'Print Preview', 'SQL View', and 'Clear Grid'. Now you can switch between views with the keyboard rather than moving your hands off the keyboard and mousing. Clear Grid is helpful when you want to get rid of everything you've put into the Query Design grid.

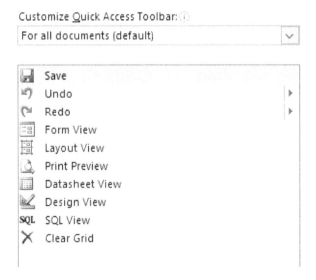

Figure 1 Adding buttons to the Quick Access Toolbar

Set Form/Report Options

We need to ensure that any code that Access generates is VBA.

Go to the Access Options menu again, and open the Access Options dialog. On the Object Designers tab, scroll to Form/Report design view. Check "Always use event procedures" as shown at the bottom of Figure 2.

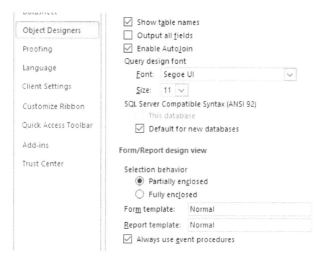

Figure 2 Form/Report design options

Use Control Wizards

The more we can get Access to do for us, the better. Therefore, let's set it so it writes code for us.

1. Activate the "Create" ribbon.

2. Click "Blank Form". A new Form opens. The ribbon shows icons of Controls in the Controls panel of the ribbon.

3. Click the dropdown of the Controls display to reveal several options. Cf. Figure 3

4. Select "Use Control Wizards"

5. Select the Home ribbon. Close and discard the Form.

Figure 3 Setting 'Use Control Wizards'

Old Forms That Don't Use VBA

...can be converted. Take this slowly, and make sure you're working on a copy of your database. This is an effort for the long haul. If you've inherited a working database, there's no need to convert parts that are working.

You can tell a Form doesn't use VBA if, when you open the Form Property Sheet, you find an event that shows that an [Embedded Macro] is responsible for handling some event.

If you need to modify the macro, you can use Access to convert that macro to VBA.

Open the Form in Design View.

In the Tools panel of the Form Design Tools | Design tab, find the Convert Forms Macros to Visual Basic. Click that button. The Convert form macros dialog opens offering two options: add error handling, and include comments. Accept both offers and click Convert. This reliable process converts

the [Embedded macro] to an [Event Procedure].
Cf. Figure 4.

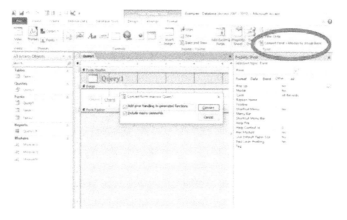

Figure 4 Convert macros to VBA

Ensure that your forms have Modules

It sometimes happens that you need to add some
code to a Form, but you can't because Microsoft
Access says the Form has to have a Module. This
language is a little loose, because what the Form
gets is a Class Module (there is a difference).

- Open the Form in **Design View**

- On the Property sheet, open the Other tab

- Set the Has Module property to Yes

Cf. Figure 5.

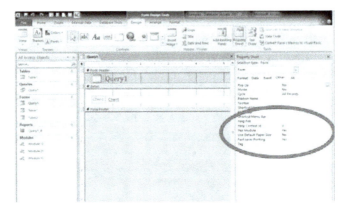

Figure 5 Set the Form Has Module property in Design view

The VBE generates a Class Module with the name 'Form_Xxxx', where 'Xxxx' is the name of your Form.

If your Form has the name 'TaxRates', the name of the Class Module will be 'Form_TaxRates'.

The VBA Environment (VBE)

VBE is the Visual Basic Environment. It's where you construct, test, and run VBA code. It's also known as the Interactive Development Environment, or IDE. It is watching every one of your keystrokes, and is anticipating what you are about to type. Microsoft calls this Intellisense, and it means you can let the VBE finish things you type by pressing Alt+Spacebar.

The first time you open up the VBE, there's a lot of blankness. Click on the View Menu, and activate in turn:

1. the Immediate window,

2. the Locals window, and

3. the Watches window.

Adjust their widths to be about equal.

Figure 6 shows this.

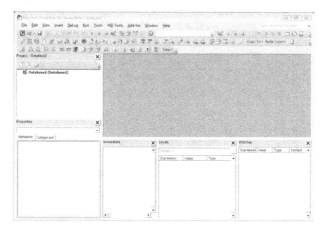

Figure 6 VBE with helpful windows

Set up the VBA code Editor

Click on Tools | Options. Set your editor options to look like Figure 7.

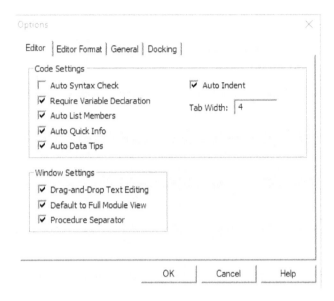

Figure 7 VBE Editor Options

We leave the Auto Syntax Check checkbox un-checked to avoid having the VBE interrupt us every time we mistype, which is often.

Check Require Variable Declaration. VBA code is organized in Modules. With this option checked, the VBE inserts the line

Option Explicit

at the top of a new module. This REQUIRES that you declare every variable in your code as to its data type. Otherwise, the VBE will allow you to misspell your variable names.*

On the General tab, set up your environment as shown in Figure 8.

The default options on the other tabs suit us. Click the Help button for a description of these options.

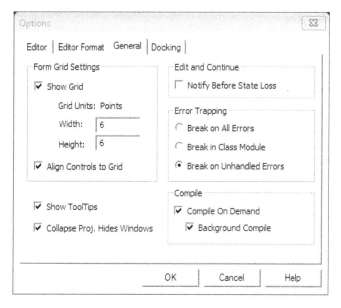

Figure 8 General VBE options

Click OK to close the Options dialog.

---

* How bad could it be? https://arstechnica.com/civis/viewtopic.php?t=862715

At this point, the VBE is 'ready', at the functionality level of the 1990s.

Your audience

Perhaps hardest to learn is "for whom do I write this code?" You are writing for yourself, and your fellow human beings. Anyone, really, who would read your code, anyone who someday inherits your code. Try to be as clear as possible. Clear code is "easy to understand". This is the aspect of writing code that's learned through practice. Practice makes perfect, but takes time. Consider this: if someone is reading the code, it means there's probably a problem. Efficiency in this case is measured in readability. You want to shorten the time it takes for the code reader (you) to understand what is staring them (you) in the face and not working. Your code reader (you) will thank you, too.

Applying the Commandments

Before you do anything else, split your Access app. When you split it, the front end will contain only the queries, forms, reports and modules. The back end will contain only the tables. This allows you to continue to work on the app independently from the data. If you have more than one user, give each of them their own copy of the front end linked to the back end. Usually, the back end is on the network server, and the front ends are on each user's desktop.

To split a database, Access provides the Access Database command on the Move Data segment of the Database Tools tab of the ribbon.

As a newbie, you're in one of three situations:

1. You have no database yet.

2. You've inherited a working database

3. You've inherited a database with problems

1. You have no database yet.

Let the commandments in this book guide you as you write new code. Be prepared to split your database when you have some of it built. The most important part of database work is getting the tables and their relations right. When that's done properly, problems are minimized.

2. You've inherited a working database

You might be tempted to rip something apart because "it wasn't done right."

THOU SHALT NOT!

Some parts are probably working now, and will continue to work as is, at least for a while. You're in a patch, splint, bind, and sometimes, cauterize, phase.

3. You've inherited a database with problems
Find out, from the users, what's not working.
Perform triage; make a plan to repair what
can be repaired. Fix what you can and get
your system somewhat stable.

MAKE A COPY OF THE DATABASE,
AND WORK WITH THE COPY.

When changes need to be made, begin following
the commandments to develop code more easily,
more cleanly, and more safely.

I. Thou Shalt Get Thee Help

This stuff is complicated! When you're stuck, open a help file! After you've launched Microsoft Access, help is available with the F1 key. Depending on your edition of Microsoft Access, you have up to four help files:

1. Database help files on your computer.

2. Database help files when you're connected to Office.com (via the internet).

3. VBA help files on your computer.

4. VBA help files when you're connected to Office.com.

Even so, you'll have questions the help files don't address, and some of the help relies on advanced knowledge. This can be opaque to a newbie. This is where the internet comes in.

Ask the internet

You're not alone! Post your question to your favorite search engine. Often, Google search will find answers to your questions from the Microsoft online help files that Microsoft itself cannot find.

In all likelihood, a search will take you to one of the following sites:

https://answers.microsoft.com/en-us/msoffice/forum

Choose Access as the Office topic.

Alternatively, try this forum:

https://social.msdn.microsoft.com/Forums/office/en-US/home?forum=accessdev

Before asking a question, search the forum questions to see if your question was answered at some point in the past.

On any forum, post your question as clearly as possible. You may be asked for clarification. Hang in there – the people on these fora are eager to help.

Passive web sites
There are many VBA websites and Youtube channels. They vary in quality. Among the better sites are:

1. http://allenbrow-ne.com/ Many free Access tips for casual users, serious developers, and programmers.

2. http://www.theaccessweb.com/ Originally set up by Microsoft Most Valuable Professionals (MVPs).

3. https://www.devhut.net/ Daniel Pineault's web site

and I've put together a site to support this book at

https://vbafornewbies.com.

Since it's new, it doesn't have the resources the other sites do.

Get books & start reading!

The best part about books is that for the price (and you should buy used books) you get the "free" code that comes with it. Because of the retro nature of VBA, you don't need the latest book. If you're not planning to make a career in the Access database field, the following are useful, but tell you more than you'll need to know.

1. *Microsoft Access 2010 VBA Programming Inside Out* by Andrew Couch (1-Aug-2011) Paperback, ISBN-13: 978-8120344594. Programming VBA up to the latest Object Oriented capabilities of VBA.

2. *Microsoft Access 2010 Programmer's Reference*, by Teresa Hennig, ISBN-13: 978-8126528127

3. Any book by Ken Getz and Paul Litwin will also be a handy book to have because of all the code you get for free.

4. You'll probably want a book or two for the database development side of things. Authors to look for include Jeff Conrad, John L. Viescas, and Phil Mitchell & Evan Callahan. Access doesn't change much from year to year, so even older books have value.

II. Thou Shalt Be Explicit

This commandment is so that the next person who must read and change the code knows to the greatest possible extent what the original purpose was. That person may be you six months after writing the code.

Therefore, you must observe the following three rules in your code:

- Every Module shall have as the first two statements

Option Compare Database
Option Explicit

- Every variable will be declared as of a specific data type.

- Every function will have a return data type specified.

These are not undue burdens, pilgrim. The VBE will write the Option Explicit code for us, as long as we have set up the environment to do so. *Intellisense* will provide most of the data types for us as choices from drop down lists. Alt+Spacebar is the keystroke.

This commandment also means that thou shalt name the pieces of thy code appropriately.

You get to name database Objects:

- Tables, Queries, Forms, Reports, and Modules

- Columns, in Tables and Queries

- Modules, where we'll put our VBA code

- Classes, another place to put our VBA code, organized a bit differently than Modules

- Variables

The Access Help Glossary gives more detail defining these entities.

If you've inherited your database, use a Reserved Word tool to scan its components. A useful one may be found at *https://www.devhut.net*. Then, change the reserved names to what is more à propos.

Such as? Aristotle said "Names are signs of ideas".

In other words, don't name things in your code after your pets. "Buffy" may be a good name for a cat, but it's (probably) a poor name of an object in a database.

Database object names

You of course have wide latitude in naming things, but you can't use the "words" of the VBA language itself to name your things. You learn the VBA vocabulary by committing syntax errors, as the VBE will point out. There are more than a few terms to avoid — more than 2,700 of them. For example: "Name" and "Date" are popular terms, but don't use them; VBA has appropriated them. Instead, modify them by including the name of the thing to which they refer, like "firstName" and "birthDate".

VBA lacks strong data typing, a characteristic that makes programs stronger. To remedy this lack, naming schemes have arisen that attempt to address the problem with a cure worse than the disease: a *Naming Convention.**

The short name for a Naming Convention is called *tibbling*. Symptoms of the disease appear as prefixing your Tables' names with *tbl* or *t*, your Queries with *qry* or *q*, etc. These prefixes come under the definition of *eyesore*, and make everything more difficult to read. Ugh! Folks afflicted with this ailment will name the *People* or *Personnel* table *tblPeople*, and their pets *dogFido* and *catBuffy*.

THOU SHALT NOT.

If you are already afflicted with this malady, cure yourself of the tibbling syndrome!

You'll find good naming advice for Tables, Queries, Forms and Reports in *Joe Celko's SQL Programming Style*, ISBN 0120887975, 2005,

---

* That is, because the VBA language isn't protecting you, you must use the language protectively, to account for the language's lacks. Naming Conventions are unenforceable.

although Joe uses the equally repugnant underscore character "_".

Well! If we can't tibble, what should we do?

Table names
Codd thought of tables as mathematical sets. If set theory is not one of your fortes, think of them as what they look like, tables with rows and columns. Table rows are in random order. Each row is supposed to be a fact. Not only that, they're supposed to be unique; no duplicates.

Name your tables for the set of objects they hold. Thus, your table names will be plural nouns. E.g., *Employees*, or *People*.

Query names
Name your queries for the effect they produce. For example, *TodaysEmployeeBirthdays* to list those employees whose birthday is today.

Form names
Name Forms for the kind of data you're trying to obtain or present. Perhaps *DisplayTodaysBirthdays*.

Report names
Name Reports for the presentation they produce. Example: *PantryVisitsInDetail*.

Columns in Tables
Do NOT include spaces in your column names, notwithstanding what you see in Microsoft

examples! If you want to make names readable, use camelCase (first character lower case).

You might have heard the idea that the '_' be substituted for a blank in a column name: don't bother. The '_' is hard to type because it requires a shift on most keyboards, and is just a pain to type and hard on the eyes.

Furthermore:

- Avoid Access reserved words.

- Avoid special characters! Use letters and numbers, only.

As an example of good names, consider the column names: *pathToDB*, *firstName*, *City*, etc.

The naming conventions above apply to the database side of the house. Now let's look at the VBA code side.

VBA object names

When you name something in a database, and in VBA, you also declare its data type. Some languages are strongly typed because once you declare a thing to be of a certain data type, the compiler makes sure you always use that thing in the manner expected. Variables, in particular, can be any type, and even change types during a program's execution.

VBA carries some of that idea today in the *Variant* data type. A *Variant* will hold anything except fixed-length String data. This includes *Empty*,

Error, *Nothing*, and *Null*. While this can be handy, the programming profession has been moving in two opposite directions simultaneously. Some languages are strongly typed and the compiler deduces the data type by the way variables are used, and some languages require NO type specifications. In our view, VBA is best when we make it as strongly typed as possible.

Give names to Modules for the calculation(s) they provide. Public procedures in a Module are always available to be called by other procedures, so they should contain calculations that are logically coherent. For example, group all date calculations in a Module called DateCalcs, or Dates; all the sine and cosine functions in Trigonometry, etc.

Insofar as Date calculations go, look around the internet or in your VBA library for procedures that are available rather than writing your own. Test them thoroughly, anyway.

Naming VBA Classes
Name Classes for their calculating object. If you're making strings, *StringBuilder* is a good Class name.

Naming Procedures
Name the calculation. Spend some time thinking of procedure names; they should be verbs, describing what they do. Conversely, what they do should match their names. Name them differently from the Module containing them!

You have a maximum of 64 characters. Please don't use all 64! I may have to read it someday. You, too!

Use CamelCase (first character upper case) to make the names legible, and to distinguish procedure names from variable names.

Some examples from the Purpose lines of our NGram Producer:

```
CollectWords - extract MSWord words
Fini - clean up
AAANGramProducer - Gather ngrams
```

Naming Variables

Name variables for what they are, using camelCase with the first character lowercase (same as column names).

VBA limits variable names to be at most 64 characters.[*] Variables that have great scope should have names befitting their grandeur. In this sense, if a Module is tracking temperatures, a module-wide variable (one available to every procedure in the Module) might have a name like roomTemp or roomTemperature.

Variables used inside a procedure, i.e., local variables, should usually be in the range of one-to-four characters in length. That's *usually*. A

---

[*] To find the limits imposed by Access, search help for "Access specifications".

temperature variable within the scope of a Function might be named *t*, or *temp*, along with a comment.

III. Thou Shalt Use Tools

We have all this computing power at our hands, so it's important to use the computer(!) in our code development!

VBA Code Assistant (VCA)

VCA is our external stand-alone tool, available at *http://vbafornewbies.com.* We use it whenever we write VBA code. Actually, VCA does most of the writing, because most of VBA is boilerplate.

More will be said about this tool as we proceed.

MZ-Tools

is at version 8.0 at the time of this writing. The tools come in a large bundle, and can be acquired at *https://www.mztools.com/index.aspx* for a nominal fee. The value of this tool is not obvious at first blink, but becomes more useful as you use it.

Caveat: You won't use all of it, because it's aimed at more than one language. It's offered as a 30-day free trial. Spend at least a day getting familiar with it.

Rubberduck

"... is a free, open-source, add-in that enhances the VBE... which was last updated well over 20 years ago." as I paraphrase the Rubberduck blog at *https://rubberduckvba.wordpress.com.* This add-in reads and analyzes your code to provide machine brainpower to what you're doing. Microsoft calls it Intellisense®; the Rubberduck team takes it up several notches. You'll feel as if the machine is helping you rather than behaving as an obstacle. The current version as of this writing is Rubberduck v2.5.0.

Caveats: Rubberduck is modern in the theories it applies to writing good code, and sort of enforces them. If you're a newbie to code, you'll learn a lot studying this tool. Use the parts that help. The size of the add-in means you'll wait a few seconds while the bits load at startup.

Because it is an add-in, it ultimately depends on Microsoft's management of the Add-in interface. Our approach is to *not rely* on add-ins, but to use them as tools.

Other

You'll find useful pieces of software in various places on the internet. The books and websites mentioned so far are good places to search.

IV. Thou Shalt Test

Edsger Dijkstra, one of the earliest software developers, said,

> *"Tests can reveal the presence of bugs, but not their absence."*

Good code depends on how good the programmer is at inventing tests to reveal (and remove) as many bugs as possible.

But wait. How do bugs get *into* our code!? Is there an enemy sowing tares in our code? No. All the bugs in the code we insert ourselves by not thinking through what we're doing.

A Development Process

One modern software development process is called Test Driven Development (TDD). The idea is that first, you write code that deliberately fails to work. Then, you fix it by writing new code, and inventing and running tests that eventually succeed. You do this until you're done.

To manage this process, elaborate software has been developed to run and record the tests. The software has names of the form *nUnit*. There is no such tool for VBA as of this writing, although there have been some attempts to build one. Rubberduck is moving in that direction.

So, we're on our own as far as test-writing goes. We don't necessarily want to learn yet another system; best is if we can stay within the confines of VBA, which we're still learning.

The simplest approach to approximate the TDD process: when you need one procedure, write *two*. The first is the procedure desired, the second is the test driver.

While it's hard enough to write one procedure, now we should double the work? No, because we have a Tool. VCA writes the procedure desired, and a test driver, so testing can begin immediately. Hardly any typing is involved. The name of the test driver is the name of the desired procedure prefixed with an X. If you want Function Foo, you get Sub XFoo to test it.

Example: the Foo function

Given the academic Foo function*

```
Public Function Foo(i As Long) As Double
'   Purpose: Foo - return 'i's Double equivalent
    Dim result As Double
    '===============================
    result = CDbl(i)   '  VBA built-in
    '===============================
    Foo = result
    Exit Function
End Function
```

---

* Foo derived from the acronym "fubar", and you're likely to see example functions in pairs named Foo and Bar.

Because Foo is Public, it is available to all other procedures in all Modules, so we won't necessarily know where it will be called from.

Part of every test is the specification of the expected result. What results do you expect from each of the tests exercised by the following Sub? Do you get what you expect?

```
Private Sub XFoo()
    Debug.Print Foo(0)
    Debug.Print Foo(-2147483648#)
    Debug.Print Foo(2147483648#)
    Debug.Print Foo(Null)
End Sub
```

What other tests would you run? Consider edge values, like zeroes, nulls, very large values, etc.

Will your code be perfect because you've tested it? Mine isn't. But it will be better than untested software. Think about this: the control of some modern aircraft is fly-by-wire. That is, control by software. Are you ready to fly in a plane controlled by your code?

V. Thou Shalt Trap

I'm going to suppose now that we have to do some kind of significant calculation. We'll need more code than a simple Function.

Trapping is all about control. The first step is to know what our calculations will produce. Trapping errors is the second step.

Code is a story

While it's not generally thought of in terms of stories, code is built along the same lines: it has a beginning, a middle, and an end.

1. The beginning is associated with the setup of those things needed to do the calculation.

2. The middle *is* the calculation.

3. The end is the post-party cleanup.

From long experience, we name these phases *Init*, *Run*, and *Fini*. Every piece of code is organized like this, although one or more of the phases might be missing, and the names of the phases might be different.

Since we know this, we can prepare a general program outline to handle our significant calculation. As our first draft, we open a new Module and write five procedures as follows:

```
Option Compare Database
Option Explicit

'    Module-wide variables
'    go here
```

```
Public Sub SigCalc()

End Sub
```

```
Private Function Init()

End Function
```

```
Private Function Run()

End Function
```

```
Private Function Fini()

End Function
```

```
Private Sub XSigCalc()

End Sub
```

Listing 1 General outline of a significant calculation

The only Public procedure is *SigCalc*, which is presumed to eventually interact with the rest of our project. Init, Run, and Fini are Private Functions, so even though they may have the same names as procedures in other Modules, they won't be accessible to them by mistake. We've sketched SigCalc here as a Sub, but if you need to use it in a Query, it must be a Function.

XSigCalc will act as the test driver for our calculation. It's important that XSigCalc be Private, because we want to test our Module in isolation.

Init, Run, and Fini are Functions. We may want each one to do some work, but we also want to know, *Did it work*? A good data type for the result is therefore Boolean. They will return True if they complete their assignments, and False if something goes wrong. They are therefore going to tell us how far our calculation has proceeded. If we successfully get through Fini, we know our calculation succeeds. Alternatively, we'll know where it fails. This is part of our Trap, because it gives us more control over our code.

All of our procedures should tell us what they do by their names. It's sometimes useful to elaborate with a comment that says what the procedure is attempting to do.

With this in mind, we revise our general outline to

```vb
Public Sub SigCalc()
' main program for significant calc
    Dim result As Boolean
    result = Init
    If result Then
        result = Run
    End If
    result = Fini(result)
End Sub
```

```vb
Private Function Init() As Boolean
    Init = False
End Function
```

```vb
Private Function Run() As Boolean
    Run = False
End Function
```

```vb
Private Function Fini(result As Boolean) As Boolean
    If result Then
        Debug.Print "Success"
    Else
        Debug.Print "Failure"
    End If
    Fini = result
End Function
```

```vb
Private Sub XSigCalc()
' test driver
    SigCalc
End Sub
```

Listing 2 Expanded outline of significant calculation

The outline in Listing 2 will compile and run as is, but its activity will be limited, as can be seen by tracing the execution path.

You can do this with the VBE by placing the cursor on the first line of XSigCalc and pressing F8 to execute each VBA statement in turn.

It can be instructive to *read* through your program. You will spend more time reading code than writing it, so you might as well start now.

At the first line of XSigCalc: execution skips over the comment. Then it skips over the Dim statement, (which *declares* the *result* variable as a Boolean[*]) and continues to the line

```
result = Init
```

which *assigns* to *result* the value returned by a call to the Init Function.

Execution transfers to the signature line[†] of Init, and moves to the first statement, which assigns the Boolean value False to Init. Execution proceeds to the End Function statement of Init, and thence back to SigCalc. There, the *result* variable is assigned the value False.

---

[*] "Dim" is short for "Dimension", borrowed from FORTRAN.

[†] The signature line shows the name of a procedure and the names and types of all the parameters that can be passed to the procedure.

Next, the If statement asks "is result true?" If the answer is yes, then execute the following statements. Otherwise, go to the End If line. Since result is False, the statements belonging to the If are skipped. Run isn't called at all.

The next statement to be executed is the call to the Fini Function, making result available to Fini. This call may look a little funny because result appears as the value returned by the function, and also in the argument list. This is all perfectly legal.

As execution proceeds through Fini, the If statement tests the value of result, finds it to be False, and so uses the Debug.Print statement to print "Failure" to the VBE Immediate Window. Execution returns SigCalc.

SigCalc runs through its End Sub statement and returns to XSigCalc.

Our program runs, but does nothing. What good is that!?

The good is that it allows us to keep running and testing our program a little piece at a time. The development process is one in which we add a few lines of code to Init. Then we add a few lines to Run. We realize we need another initialization, so we go back to Init and add it. At all times, the code compiles and runs. If it doesn't work, you broke it! But you know it was the last thing you changed that was the cause of the break. The fix to be applied is in your mind, because you've been thinking about this little piece of code.

During this process, you add variables to the Module. You insert them in between the Option Explicit statement and the first procedure in the Module. Declare them Private, even though they are Private by default. They are available to every procedure in the Module, but are independent of every other variable in the program. As they are global to the Module, they need not be passed around in argument lists.

For example, suppose we're going to make use of the data in our database.

```
Option Compare Database
Option Explicit

Private db As DAO.Database
'
'   ...
'
Private Function Init()
    Set db = CurrentDb
    Init = True
End Function
```

This code declares the object db to be a Module-wide variable, and the Init Function initializes the object to the current database.

Trapping Errors

What is an "error"?

An error is an unexpected behavior. They have been called by all the following names, among others:

- Bugs

- Errors

- Exceptions

- Flaws

- Mistakes

Captain Grace Hopper said there was a "bug" in her program when a moth flew into the case of a mainframe computer and shorted out a circuit. VBA refers to them all as Errors.

Good programming practice is to have no unexpected behaviors. But since the human mind is finite, it is near impossible to eliminate Errors. Anyway, the desire is to eliminate them as much as possible. When they do occur, catch them and deal with them.

What usually happens when there is an unprocessed error is that execution stops with an error message. While these messages might tell programmers something, they are often opaque to program users. Refer to Commandment I when error messages are opaque to you. Errors reduce your users' confidence in the software.

To deal with errors in VBA, we build a basket around the interior of a procedure. We use three facilities built into the language:

- Go to statements (with backward jumps)

- Labeled statements

- An error handler

GoTo statements

While it might look like 'go toe', the pronunciation is 'go tu'.

You're probably familiar with paper forms that say things like "If you're a Renter, go to question 5". This is the kind of thing that a VBA GoTo statement does. Rather than move attention to a different part of a paper form, it moves execution focus to a different part of the code.

GoTos were all we had in the beginning. They closely mimicked what was happening with machine instructions. We used the dickens out of them until Edsger Dijkstra's letter entitled *Go To Statement Considered Harmful* was published in the March 1968 Communications of the ACM. The result is that language designers offer synonyms for GoTo that must be used in severely constrained circumstances. A helpful VBA GoTo is spelled Resume.

The thinking in the industry gradually concluded that GoTo statements were OK as long as the direction of the Go was forward. Backward GoTos were to be avoided because it was too hard to see where the program flow was going. So: *GoTo forward* is OK, *GoTo backwards* is to be avoided, except in the case of handling errors.

Labeled statements

In the beginning days of BASIC, every program line was numbered serially by tens, thus creating the problem of line number management. When you needed to insert eleven lines of code somewhere in the middle, you had to renumber the following lines yourself. VBA eliminated the need for line numbers. Yay! That fixes *that* management problem!

But WAIT! Without line numbers, how do I know where to direct my GoTo statements!?

The "fix" is a Labeled statement, which looks like this:

```
label1:
'   this is a comment
```

Now we can write "GoTo label1", and the execution will branch from the Goto statement to the line with Label1, and continue from there. (Forward good Backward bad).

An Error handler?

Using an error handler, the idea is to catch errors and do something reasonable with the unexpected situation. With a truly unexpected situation, really, what can you do? This is why testing is so important: it is desirable to expect everything and anything. If you can expect disasters, you don't need an error handler, you write disaster expectant code. We don't have enough experience for that, so there will be errors.

Start the Error Handler

This is more easily seen with some code. I'll start with the *Init* function, revised as shown in Listing 3.

```
Private Function Init() As Boolean
    On Error GoTo errorExit
    Dim result As Boolean
    result = False
    '==============================
    '  your calculation here
    '==============================
    Init = result

End Function
```

Listing 3 Init function without error handling

The *On Error* statement directs the compiler in the event of an error to create *Err*, an object of the Error Class. The clause *GoTo errorExit* says that the next statement to be executed after an error occurs will be the one labeled *errorExit*. We'll add that in a moment.

In our procedures, we declare a (redundant) variable *result* into which we'll put the truth about our calculation progress. We set it to False immediately. Using *result* to hold any intermediate results allows us to avoid accidental recursion, which is beyond the scope of this book.

After *your calculation*, in which we may set the value of result to *True*, we assign the value of result to the function. We then run off the end of the function at the *End Function* statement and return to the calling procedure.

Add Labeled Statements and GoTos to Catch Errors

The best place for us to catch Err is at the bottom of our function, like this;

```
errorExit:
    Debug.Print err.Description
    Stop

End Function
```

Listing 4 Error handler, first draft

and the errorExit will be the target of the On Error statement.

Thus, if there is an error, execution jumps to the labeled statement errorExit and continues. The Debug.Print statement writes the error description to the immediate window.

Stop comes next. Execution stops, awaiting your manual intervention. If you continue execution from this point, you will step to the End Function statement and exit to the calling function.

This is obviously the error handler for development only; stopping a program in your user's hands will subject you, your ancestors, and your heritage to curse. What we have written here is an error fumbler, rather than a handler. We'll discuss true handlers in a bit.

You might've noticed a problem with this idea: if there is no error, the code still runs through the error fumbler and stops. We don't want that. Instead, we need some code to avoid the error fumbler when there is no error.

There's also the problem of cleaning up after the calculation that this error has subverted. We really want to exit this function at one place, which would be our defined exit, not just running off the end. Therefore, we define our own exit and fix it with yet another labeled statement as follows:

```
exitProcessing:
    On Error Resume Next
    Init = result
    Exit Function
```

Listing 5 Defining the single exit point of a function

In Listing 5, The statement *On Error Resume Next* tells the error processing code to ignore any more errors. That is, we're shutting the error processing off for the rest of this function. The value of result is assigned to the function, and we exit.

When you're developing code, Stop is helpful. But on occasion, we would like to return to the scene of the crime to determine what the problem *IS*. For this purpose, we use two cloaked GoTos:

- Resume labeledstatement

- Resume

We extend Listing 4 as follows:

```
errorExit:
  Debug.Print err.Description
  Stop
  Resume exitProcessing
  Resume

End Function
```

Listing 6 Error handler, second draft

where we've inserted the undesirable backward goto *Resume exitProcessing*.

This code works like this: We land on Stop when there's an error and try to figure out what VBE is telling us about our program. If we continue execution by pressing F8, execution flows to the Resume exitProcessing statement. In the next step, execution continues at the statement labeled *exitProcessing*.

Then again, if we instead *select* the plain *Resume* statement, and then press Ctrl+F9, execution flows to the line that caused the error. By hovering the mouse over our variables, we can see their values in pop-up windows. We can use the Immediate window to set the values of variables that we think caused the error and resume our testing.

One other effect of the Resume statements that differs from GoTo statements: a Resume clears the error. Philosophically, this follows the idea of subsidiarity, which says that problems that arise should be dealt with as closely to the source as possible, by the people on the scene.

The Transformed Init

After our error handling additions, our *Init* Function looks like this

```
Private Function Init() As Boolean
    On Error GoTo errorExit
    Dim result As Boolean
    result = False
    '==============================
    '   your calculation here
    '==============================
exitProcessing:
    On Error Resume Next
    Init = result
    Exit Function


errorExit:
    Debug.Print err.Description
    Stop
    Resume exitProcessing
    Resume


End Function
```

Listing 7 Procedure fitted with error handling

Considerations

You look this over and realize that the original three-line Init has swelled to nineteen lines! That seems like a lot more code than you want to type, and you're right. It's a lot more code than I want to type, too. Once again, let us consider Tools that write code.

One way is to use the macro processor in MZTools to write this code for you. The disadvantage is that you have to learn yet another language to describe what you want the tool to do. We're not interested in learning yet another language at this time, thank you.

A simpler approach is to use the standalone program VCA. In our practice, we launch it so that it sits on the desktop ready for use. Then, for each Function, we

- Use the Windows keystroke Alt+Tab to change the focus from the VBE to VCA;

- Select the Function radio button by pressing Alt+F (every option has an accelerator key);

- Press Alt+N to move to the Name textbox;

- Fill in the name of the Function desired;

- Press Alt+D to move to the Description textbox;

- Enter some descriptive text (please do);

- Press Alt+G to Generate the code which is saved to the Clipboard;

- Press Alt+Tab to return to the VBE;

- Press Ctrl+V to insert the code in the Module.

This is not onerous: you get a whole Function with error traps for nine keystrokes in addition to the name and description of the Function. your hands haven't left the keyboard once.

True Error Handlers

While the fumbler is good enough for development work, or for your own private databases, projects that will be released require something a bit stronger, perhaps something like

```
errorExit:
    ErrorReport Err, "Init", Erl
    Resume exitprocessing
    Resume
```

in which ErrorReport is a global Sub, Err is the error object, Init is the procedure in which the error occurred, and Erl is the line number at which the error occurred[*]. The ErrorReport procedure can perhaps store the error information in an *Errors* table, along with the name of the user who was operating the database, the date, time, etc.

Further study

Check the Err object in VBA Help.

------

[*] Use MZTools to number the lines of your code if you go this route.

VI. Thou Shalt Trace

Obeying Commandments I through V will help us produce safe, understandable, and reliable code. Yet, more monitoring and diagnosis is possible, and therefore, desirable.

A *Trace* is a list of the procedures executed during the current calculation. Such a list is trivial when only one procedure is involved, but when the Init, Run, and Fini procedures call other procedures, it's worth knowing what's going on.

Trace grew out of a set of procedures I wrote in Fortran in the 1980s and implemented on several mainframes.

While VBA provides the call stack of executing code at some instant when you've hit a Stop statement (press Ctrl+L), it doesn't provide a history. If we look at the safe and reliable Init Function once again, we'd like to have something like

```
Private Function Init() As Boolean
    On Error GoTo errorExit
    Debug.Print "Enter Init"
    Dim result As Boolean
    result = False
    '===============================
    ' your calculation here
    '===============================
exitProcessing:
    On Error Resume Next
    Init = result
    Debug.Print "Leave Init"
    Exit Function

errorExit:
    Debug.Print Err.Description
    Stop
    Resume exitProcessing
    Resume
End Function
```

Every time Init is executed, the Debug.Print statement writes the Enter and Leave message to the Immediate window unless something fails and you enter the Error fumbler. If you are at the Stop, look at the Immediate window and you'll know what procedure you're in and how you got there.

Yes, we want something like that, but not exactly. The idea is to put this functionality in a separate Module.

Specifications

At a bare minimum, we want

1. Each procedure name output to the VBE Immediate window as control flow enters the procedure, and as it leaves.

2. Each output procedure name should be indented by one space from the name of the caller, and outdented upon return.

3. Implemented as a Module, rather than a Class, so it can be used in an ad hoc manner. That is, we can start calling Trace procedures without any setup.

4. The Module shall be called Trace.

This is a sufficient to get us started. By separating this functionality into a separate Module, we can make changes to the Trace code without messing up our program.

Trace methods

Enter(procName as String)

will be called as the first executable statement in a procedure in place of the Debug.Print.

Leave(procName as String)

will be called as the last executable statement of a procedure. This is why a single exit from a procedure is **mandatory**.

First Draft

We already know how to write to the Immediate window using Debug.Print, and we'll keep using that. The tricky part will be tracking the indent and outdent.

```
Option Compare Database
Option Explicit

Const MAXINDENT As Long = 10
Private m_Indent    As Long
```

```
Public Sub Enter(procName As String)
   Debug.Print Space(m_Indent) & _
      "Enter " & procName
   IncreaseIndent
End Sub
```

```
Public Sub Leave(procName As String)
   DecreaseIndent
   Debug.Print Space(m_Indent) & _
      "Leave " & procName
End Sub
```

Listing 8 Basic Trace procedures

The internal variable *m_Indent* will keep track of indenting and outdenting. To indicate that variables are internal, we'll prefix them with *m_*.*

---

* Yeah, I know I said I don't like underscores, but this exception to the rule is common in languages other than VBA.

Space() is a built-in VBA function that returns a String of m_Indent blank characters. m_Indent starts out as 0, because that's what VBA sets everything to at the start of execution. Therefore, the first call to Enter will have an indent of 0.

The "&" character means "String concatenation", so the string that will be output will look like

```
(m_indent * space)Enter procname
```

Of course, we need some code for the *IncreaseIndent* and *DecreaseIndent* procedures.

IncreaseIndent

IncreaseIndent needs to increase the indent, and guard against pushing things out the window to the right if the indent gets too large. That's the reason for the constant

```
Const MAXINDENT As Long = 10
```

at the top of the file, and we'll use that as a control on indenting. It's a lot easier to read code that describes the purpose of "10" rather than to sprinkle magic numbers through a Module. Constants are Private by default.

After thinking this through, IncreaseIndent should: increase the indent by 1, but not exceed MAXINDENT. Our code looks like this

```
Private Sub IncreaseIndent()
   m_Indent = Min(m_Indent + 1, MAXINDENT)
End Sub
```

Listing 9 IncreaseIndent complete

Min will be a function that returns the minimum of two Longs, so the single statement in this procedure says "Add 1 to m_Indent, and compare that to MAXINDENT. Return the minimum of those, and set m_Indent to that value."

While SQL has a Min function, VBA doesn't! So, we'll write that in a moment.

DecreaseIndent

DecreaseIndent will be the mirror image of IncreaseIndent. This time, we don't want to run off the window to the left, so the most DecreaseIndent can decrease to is 0.

With this in mind, the code looks like this

```
Private Sub DecreaseIndent()
   m_Indent = Max(m_Indent - 1, 0)
End Sub
```

Listing 10 DecreaseIndent complete

Max is a function that returns the maximum of two Longs. The single line of code in this Sub says "subtract 1 from m_Indent and compare that to 0. Assign the maximum of those two to m_indent."

VBA doesn't provide Max, either, so we'll write Min and Max now.

Min & Max

Min and Max are two functions that wrap If...Else statements. Here are both of them.

```
Private Function Min(a As Long, b As Long) As Long
   If a <= b Then
      Min = a
   Else
      Min = b
   End If
End Function
```

```
Private Function Max(a As Long, b As Long) As Long
   If a >= b Then
      Max = a
   Else
      Max = b
   End If
End Function
```

Listing 11 Min and Max functions

We now have a functional Trace Module.

Sticking in calls in the now safe and reliable Init function, the change is hardly visible

```
Private Function Init() As Boolean
    On Error GoTo errorExit
    Enter "Init"
    Dim result As Boolean
    result = False
    '===============================

    '===============================
exitProcessing:
    On Error Resume Next
    Init = result
    Leave "Init"
    Exit Function

errorExit:
    Debug.Print Err.Description
    Stop
    Resume exitProcessing
    Resume

End Function
```

Calls to Trace are most easily inserted when your procedures are generated by a tool; hence, VCA again.

An extended version of Trace is in Appendix C.

Why no error handling in this Module!?

There is no need for error code because all the data is interior to the Module, and the only way to access it is through the interface, which restricts everything to a set of known values. It is of course worthy of thorough testing.

Where to put this code?

Trace is a useful extension to the Access working environment, but who wants to write it more than once? Therefore, it should be stored somewhere outside the current database so you can use it on more than one project. See Commandment IX: Thou Shalt Archive Modules for the way to do this.

VII. Thou Shalt Distribute Form Code

Forms have three jobs:

- to **support** users to access and change the database, and

- to **prevent** users from accessing and changing the database tables and queries directly, and

- to **prevent** users from accessing and changing the database incorrectly.

Forms are designed to do the first two of these easily. The third issue involves strict vetting of the data your users enter in the form. What we're looking for are the seams along which it's easy to split the functionality of Forms. We want our development process to work smoothly, and, our software to work properly as well

The mindset to adopt is that everything coming in from the keyboard are evil bits intent on destroying the database. This leads to a form generation process in which, if possible, your users get combo boxes from which to select among legal alternatives, rather than have them mistype their data entries.

You want to prevent your users from acting directly with the tables, queries, and code.* Even so, there will be times when your users need to type in data. Your rôle then becomes one of writing error detecting (and possibly correction) code to ensure that your business rules are observed. When type-ins are necessary, test them for reasonability. Ask for verification if you don't think it's reasonable.

Writing code for a Form

In order to write VBA code for a form, it must have a module. Open the form in Design View. Open the Property Sheet and select the Form as the selection type. Open the 'Other' tab, and set 'Has Module' to 'Yes'.

---

* Depending on the situation, it may be desirable to keep user hands off other parts of the interface, like the Navigation pane and the Ribbon. Check "Options for the current database", and Help, to restrict access thereto.

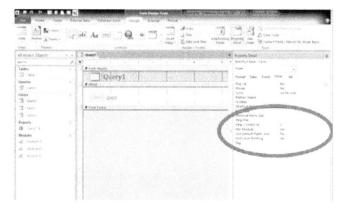

Figure 9 How to add a module

Control Wizards?

But suppose you've used the Control Wizards, and Access wrote macro code for you? (Here I mean the macro code to be avoided.) Open the Form in Access Design View. In the Tools panel, click 'Convert Form's Macros to Visual Basic'. (cf. Figure 10 Converting Macros to VBA). Check to add error handling and include comments, at your pleasure. Click Convert.

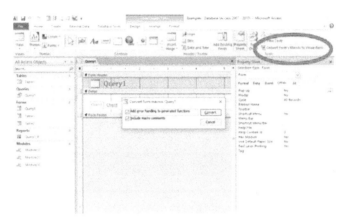

Figure 10 Converting Macros to VBA

That gets us a Module behind the Form, the schematic view of which is shown in Figure 11

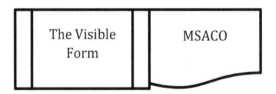

Figure 11 Form and Microsoft Access Class Object

The Module, labeled as MSACO, is the **M**icro**s**oft
Access **C**lass **O**bject that goes with this form. The
graphical **Form**, and the textual **Class Object**, are
tightly coupled.

While the juncture of The Visible Form and the
MSACO may appear to be a useful seam, It Isn't.
Access manages the connection, and it's best to
let it.

Because of the tight coupling, you might be tempted to put everything possible into that MSACO. Don't, because Access sometimes has problems. When you make too many changes at one time* with the Form open, you may be on the receiving end of this action by Access. It

- issues an error message,

- says that it's closing the database,

- closes it,

- reopens it, and

- poof! your latest code is gone along with changes in the Form.

You are encouraged when this happens ... to pray for the Microsoft programmers.

To guard against loss of work, compile often, save often, and compact & repair often.

We don't want to lose work, yet we want to ensure that everything is tested. So, don't put everything in the MSACO. Rather, think of the Form as a facade hiding the code for your significant calculation which will be done in a separate Module. In some cases, we'll need some code to connect the Form and the Module, which means we might have four parts to our Form.

---

* An indeterminate number.

Four parts of a Form

What's hard to see in Figure 11 are the seams
where the software easily separates into the appropriate parts. Use these rules

1. You are limited to three kinds of code in
    the MSACO:

    a. event code (reacting to something
        happening on the GUI Form, like
        the OnClick event of a button);

    b. thorough data checking and error
        prevention code of user input; and

    c. code to set up the Connector Ob-
        ject, with a call to Tested Code.

2. Any code that needs testing is in another
    module, which you have tested to death
    with test software.

3. Finally, it may be necessary to write a
    Class module to connect the MSACO to the
    calculation Module.

These ideas result in four parts for each Form

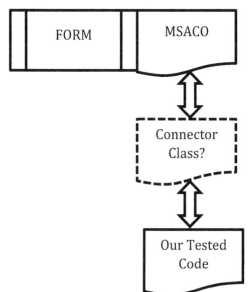

Figure 12 Four parts of a Form

How to name the Four Parts

Access takes your Form name as a prefix, and names the MSACO in such a way as to indicate the tight relationship. So if you've created a Form *Qtr-Stats* to deal with statistics for the latest quarter, Access will name the MSACO *Form_QtrStats*. It's best to not willy-nilly change the names of things in the MSACO, because Access is doing the managing.

A suggested name for Our Tested Code in this case would be *QtrStatsCalc*.

Finally, should we need one, the Connector Object
could be called *QtrStatsConn*.

How to Write the Parts

The OurTestedCode Module
Develop your significant calculations independently of the Form, in a separate Module, using what's called mock, or fake, data. Test this
code to death. When the tests are done, the mock
data doesn't need to be removed, but rather can
be turned into comments by placing an apostro-
phe in the first column.

The code in this module will look something like
this

```
Dim ClientID As Long
Dim lastName As String
    Etc.
```

```
Public Sub QtrStatsMainProgram(arglist)
    Dim result As Boolean
    result = Init
    If result Then
        Run
    End If
    result = Fini (result)
End Sub
```

```
Private Sub XDevQtrStatsMainProgram()
    Dim result As Boolean
    ClientID = 123
    lastName = 'Bohunka'
    '   put data into arglist
    QtrStatsMainProgram arglist
End Sub
```

Etc. (code for Init, Run, Fini omitted)

Listing 12 Dev code for QtrStatsCalc

In Listing 12, use *XDevQtrStatsMainProgram* (the last Sub shown) to run *QtrStatsMainProgram* using data that tests the calculation independent of the Form.

The MSACO

Assuming the Form has checked all the incoming data, the problem is getting data to and from the

module. At some point in the execution of the
Form, you will make the call to OurTestedCode by
forming the arglist as shown in Listing 12, and
calling QtrStatsMainProgram exactly as does our
test driver XDevQtrStatsMainProgram.

Forming the arglist

There are three obvious ways to construct an arglist.

A desirable quality is that it be short. In this con-
text, short means (while waving my hands) from
none to four variables. This makes it easier to ensure that you're passing the proper values to the
proper parameters, and not switching Doubles
for Strings. The compiler will check this, but if
you use Variants, anything is legal, so you have to
get this right. That is the first and simplest way,
by direct substitution of values in the arglist.

The second way to pass arguments is to use a
thing called the ParamArray, in which all of the
arguments are of type Variant. If you use only the
ParamArray to pass arguments, it minimizes the
arglist size to one. A ParamArray also allows hel-
ter-skelter ordering of variables in the list, so you
have to get this right, too.

A third way is to construct an Object, which requires a bit of effort, but which guarantees that
the types always match. It also minimizes arglist
size to one.

To discover how to build a simple Object, see
Commandment VIII.

VIII. Thou Shalt Use Objects

There are five basic aspects of VBA Object knowledge, under these headings:

- What is an Object

- Microsoft's Classes and Objects

- How to Use Classes

- How to Write Classes

- How to Use Your Classes and objects

What is an Object?

An object is code that's made according to the pattern defined by the Class. You might think of a Class as an elaborate data Type.

Classes are Modules that are organized differently from the standard VBA Module. In the standard VBA Module, all the (Public) code is available to every other Module all the time.

In the Class Module, you

- Define data that is ideally, and deliberately, concealed from public view.*

- Define Methods that operate on the data.

---

* Experience shows that this is A Good Thing®.

- Define Properties that operate on the data
  and modify VBA syntax.

Classes are like Modules, and in the VBE, they're
even referred to as "Class Modules". All the code
inside a Class is VBA.

But the Class is a pattern, or a template, or a
Type. In order to use the Class you need to "make
an Object" of that Type, just as when you declare
a variable to be a String, say. And just like Strings,
you can make as many Objects as you need. This
comes in handy when you need several Objects of
the same type to perform a calculation. The sur-
prising thing about Objects is that through compiler tricks, they each have their own data and
share code.

Microsoft's Classes and Objects

In the VBE, open help. Type "access object model"
in the search box. It will take some time to learn
the whole object model. What we're looking for is
kind of a casual acquaintance with it, rather than
a thorough knowledge. I recommend starting at
the Application Object. Focus on DAO (Data Access Objects) rather than the ADO (Access Data
Objects), which is "sort of deprecated" by Microsoft. The rumor is that they're not developing
it any further. Good practice in this case is to go
where Microsoft's action is, and that's DAO. But, if
your inherited database code is written using

ADO, don't switch until you understand it. That's beyond the scope of this text.

Using Microsoft Classes

The steps to use a Microsoft Class:

- Declare an Object as an instance of a Class

- Open the Object using a Class Method.

- Use the Object to perform a calculation

- Dispose of the Object.

It's important to Dispose of objects you make by setting the object to Nothing. If you don't deliberately do this, *usually* VBA will do it for you when you exit a procedure. But when you're writing some code, and executing it several times in tests, you may restart with some ghost objects left over. If you're testing, therefore, it's wise to press "Reset", and compile again before you restart. Good practice is to dispose of an object when you're done with it, like this

```
set yourobject = Nothing
```

The VBA to use a Recordset Class will look like this:

```
Dim rst As Recordset   ' declare
Set rst = Currentdb.OpenRecordset( "QueryOrTable", _
        dbOpenDynaset)   ' open

… some calculation using rst

rst.Close
Set rst = Nothing      ' dispose
```

Listing 13 Class calculation pattern

In Listing 13, *Recordset* is a Microsoft Class, whereas *rst* is an Object.

Making an Object is a two-statement process: Declare the type of each object using the Dim statement. Then use the Set statement to assign the Class code to the Object per Listing 13. You may run into language elsewhere in which this is called "making an Instance of the Class". It's also called "newing up an object".

One of my common mistakes is to forget to use Set. Instead of

```
Dim rst As Recordset
Set rst = CurrentDb. etc
```

I'll write

```
Dim rst As Recordset
rst = CurrentDb. oto
```

When VBA tries to execute my code, it throws an error* with the remark

Object variable or With block variable not set

Each Class may have Properties and Methods

- Properties hide the data of the Object, while simultaneously making controlled access possible.

- Methods are Subs and Functions that act on the data associated with an Object. In standard VBA Modules, I call Subs and Functions *procedures.*

- Special Methods called Events respond to actions, like keystrokes, mouse movements and clicks, etc. These are part of the Microsoft Access interface.

The Class organization is a good way to *isolate* parts of a program from other parts, and the compiler supports it. With this organization, code in one part of a program doesn't mess up another part of the program. We've discovered that isolation and independence are A Good Thing®, and Classes improve on the use of Public and Private. I've said that before, but it's worth repeating.

---

* This is known as a "run-time error" because it is found when the program is running. "Compile-time" errors are found when the compiler analyzes the code.

How to Write Classes

Using Classes in VBA is straightforward per Listing 13. *Writing* Classes is a bit more intricate, and
the VBE offers only a little help in this regard. As
an example, for this section, I'll write a Class to
build strings, which I'll call *StringBuilder*.

When a Class is involved, the VBE changes subtly,
and produces different things.

Class changes to the VBE

In the VBE, the Insert menu offers a way to insert
a new Class into your project:

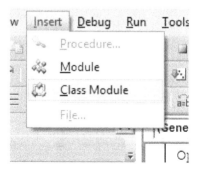

Figure 13 Inserting a Class Module

The VBE opens the window containing our standard startup text

```
(General)

    Option Compare Database
    Option Explicit

    |
```

Figure 14 The beginnings of a Class

So far, nothing new.

But in the object window [directly above the code window where it says (General)], clicking the down arrow reveals the new VBE feature.

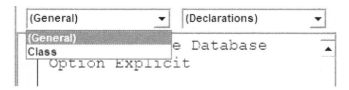

Figure 15 Class added to the Object window

With Class selected in the Object window, click on the down arrow of the (Declarations) window, and the VBE adds a Private Sub

```
Class                    ▼    Initialize              ▼

    Option Compare Database                              ▲
    Option Explicit

    Private Sub Class_Initialize()
    |
    End Sub
```

Figure 16 Object startup code

Clicking again in the (Declarations) window
shows another procedure, Terminate. Click that
to add it to the Class Module code.

```
Class

    Option Compare Database
    Option Explicit

    Private Sub Class_Initialize()

    End Sub

    Private Sub Class_Terminate()

    End Sub
```

Figure 17 Object Startup and Shutdown Procedures

You can use these two procedures to set start up
values, and to clean up when it's time for the object to die.

They have a few problems, though:

- They're Private, and therefore you can't
  call them from outside the Class unless
  you make them Public.

- They're optional. If you don't insert any
  code in them, the VBE removes them from
  your Class code. Well, that's (supposedly)
  also true of any other codeless procedure,
  so if you want to preserve an empty procedure in your code, make sure it contains
  at least a comment.

- Their names are a bit kludgy; they really should be Object_Initialize, since they don't initialize anything for the Class, but rather for the Objects that are made from the Class. Nonetheless, it's also useful to know we're starting an Object from scratch, so I will use Class_Initialize for StringBuilder.

- VBA runs Class_Initialize in the background when you new up an object. It runs Class_Terminate when an object goes away.

- Conclusion: we'll have to write our own Initialize and Terminate procedures if we need to do something more elaborate.

The Class Name

The name of the Class is defined by the name of the Class Module. The VBE doesn't know our intent, so when we add a Class to our project, it names them sequentially Class1, Class2, etc. For more meaning in our code, go to the Properties window and change the Name [on the line next to (Name)] from Class1 to StringBuilder; Cf. Figure 18

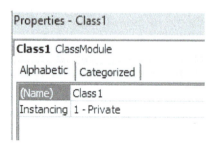

Figure 18 Changing the Class Name

Fields

Each of the hidden data entities of an Object is called a Field. For each Field, there are two Properties:

- one to assign a value to the field (the Let property), and

- one to return the value of the field (the Get property).

But you're not limited to simple assignment; you can stick a calculation in either of these Properties if needed.

Fields can be Public, but the need for such a condition is so rare as to be non-existent. Instead, make all Fields Private.

Properties

Classes give you the opportunity to hide the Fields so other Modules can't change their values directly. The VBA mechanism for this is Properties. Properties allow access to the Fields through an interface that protects the variable, while also allowing calculations to produce required return values.

Properties look like Functions, so the syntax to retrieve a Property from an Object is the "=" sign to assign the value, and the "." (the *dot*, or period) to associate the field with the Object. You interact with an object by setting or retrieving properties, or by invoking methods. The methods may be Functions or Subs. The syntax for all of these is to use the object name followed by a period "." followed by the property or method name.

Therefore, with a Stringbuilder Class, we use a Stringbuilder Object like this

```
Dim sb As StringBuilder    '  declare
Set sb = New StringBuilder    '  "new up"
sb.Append "SELECT * FROM "    '  use the object
'  etc.
Debug.Print sb.TheString
Set sb = Nothing    '  done with object
```

That's what the Class looks like from the programmer's point of view. From the developer's point of view it looks like this

```
Option Compare Database
Option Explicit

Private m_String As String

Public Property Get TheString() As String
    TheString = m_String
End Property

Public Property Let TheString(ByVal vNewValue As String)
    m_String = vNewValue
End Property

Public Sub Append(aString As String)
    m_String = m_String & aString
End Sub

Private Sub Class_Initialize()
    m_String = vbNullString\
End Sub
```

Listing 14 The Stringbuilder Class

What's new in Listing 14 are the words "Property
Get" where you might expect to see "Function",
and "Property Let" where you might expect to see
"Sub". The Class is narrowly focused on dealing
with Strings. If the Class is an interface to a table
in which Nulls are possible, the arguments to the
properties will be Variants to allow this.

The *Append* Method is a Sub. Because it's part of
the Class, it has access to the data hidden in the
Object.

Note that the only way to access the field
m_String (the internal variable) from outside the
Object is through the Properties and the Methods.

How to Use Your Objects

The general rules for using a Class is the four-step
process:

- Declare an Object of the Class type.

- "New up" the Object. This is the difference
  between Your objects and Microsoft's:
  you must use the word "New" for your objects, whereas Microsoft's objects are
  "available".

- Use the Object in a calculation.

- Destroy the Object, returning the resources to the system.

Discussion

- How do I know what the StringBuilder
  Class offers me? The VBE provides the
  Object Explorer, activated by the F2 key.
  F2 shows us there's

  ▪ a Private "field" named m_String,

  ▪ the signature of the Public Append
    method

  ▪ the signature of TheString prop-
    erty.

Why not just put all this code into a Module? For perhaps the greatest reason to use Classes/Instances: You can use multiple independent Objects of the same Class simultaneously. VBA classes are useful to define independent calculations, and they can be tested independently, as well. In their relation to database tables, objects can hold pieces of data until a full row has been accumulated, and a SQL INSERT can be executed.

Solving One Problem of Classes

Obviously, VBA classes require a *lot* of boilerplate code. In order to make classes useful, therefore, we need a *tool* to generate all that boilerplate. I'll call the tool AccessClassBuilder.

While generating such a tool, I want to minimize the amount of work I have to do. I translate this into "produce as few forms in this app as possible." And "use as much stuff already lying around" so I don't have to make much other stuff, either.

Tool Interface

I'll use the Access "Create Table Dialog".

Field Names will become the Property Names
Therefore, no spaces are allowed in field names.

- No Attachment fields
- No Lookup fields
- No Calculated fields

The tool won't deal with unrecommended data types, nor will it deal with fields that are objects or classes.*

Data Types for the Properties

Because Nulls are possible in databases, the Get and Let properties will take in and return the backing fields as *Variants*, respectively.

The Description column of the table design grid is ignored.

Tool Output

- A *.cls file in the directory of the database whose filename = tableName & "SQL.cls"
- All fields, in alphabetical order.
- All Get & Let properties, in alphabetical order.
- Class_Initialize, setting all fields to Null.
- A SQL INSERT string to insert all of the properties into the table. Autonumber

---

* Note: If you're building a Class that doesn't interface with a table, use a throw-away table to define the fields.

fields are not inserted. If you won't use
this, throw it away.

Availability
AccessClassBuilder is available free of charge
from the website vbafornewbies.com.

IX. Thou Shalt Archive Modules

We can test our code by stepping through each statement with the F8 key. With Trace engaged, every time we encounter an Enter or Leave statement, execution enters the Trace Module and steps through the code there. After awhile this gets to be painful, because the Trace module has been thoroughly tested. We don't need to see all the calls that Trace is making to its procedures. Although we need the Trace output, we don't want to visit the Trace module. Archiving the Trace Module will automatically step over all the Trace code.

Our goal is to put all of our support code into a database called *Support.accdb*, and thence into *Support.accd***e**.

Assuming that the database you're working with is called "Working.accdb", the steps to do this:

- Create a new database called "Support"
- Import code into Support
- Compile the code
- Make a backup copy of Support
- Save the database as an ACCDE
- Set Support as a Reference

Create a new database called "Support"

Open Access without specifying a database. From the New menu, select the Blank database type. Name it "Support" and save it in your working folder (so it's easy to find. You can move it later).

Using the Access File menu, open Options. On the Current Database tab, fill in the Application Title as "Support". Set any other options you desire.

Import code into Support

The task now is to import Modules from the Working database to the Support database.

- **In the Support database**, open the "External" Data ribbon and Click "Access". Browse to the folder where your Working database resides and select it.

- Make sure the Radio button for "Import" is checked. Click OK. The Import Objects dialog opens.

- Open the Modules tab. All user Modules are listed alphabetically. Select the Modules you want to import into Support. Click OK.

- Access asks if you want to save these import steps. Click "Close", which says No to Access.

You now have a Support database that has nothing in it but VBA and its own management tables. At this point, you can remove the Trace module from Working.accdb.

Compile the code

In Support.accdb, open the VBE. Click Debug | Compile. Fix any errors (there shouldn't be any). Click Save. Close the VBE. Compact & Repair the database from File | Info.

Make a backup copy of Support.

This is crucial. If you fail to do this step, YOU MAY LOSE YOUR CODE.

Use Windows Explorer to make and save a copy of Support.accdb.

Make an executable file

On the Support database File | Save & Publish tab, select "Make ACCDE", and click Save. This creates the file *Support.accde*. The VBA in this file is locked and unviewable. But the Public procedures in the file are available! We just have to tell Access where they are, and we do that by including our executable as a Reference. Close Support.accde.

Set Support as a Reference

Back to the Working database. Open the VBE. In the Tools menu, click References. The References dialog opens.

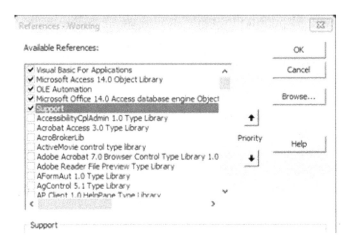

Use the Browse button to find and select the
Support.accde file. Use the dropdown and look
through "All files" to find it. Access will add
Support at the bottom of the list of Available
References, and in subsequent openings of the
dialog, it will appear near the top with the other
Available References.

X. Thou Shalt Archive Classes

Similarly to stepping through Modules whilst testing, stepping through Objects can become equally painful. Therefore it's useful to archive the Class code in an executable database. This way we stop wasting time tracing into code that is already well tested.

To do this, we need to:

- Change a Class property

- Create an Object Factory

Change a Class property

We're changing the Class so that we're not tracing into it, but that hides it from VBE. To reveal it so we can call into it, we need to change the Instancing property:

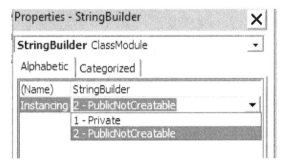

Figure 19 VBE Property window

The Instancing property must be PublicNotCreatable.

Create an Object Factory

It's much easier than it sounds. An Object Factory is a Function in a normal Module that returns an Object. To do this for Stringbuilder, the Function looks like this:

```
Public Function NewStringBuilder()As StringBuilder
   Set NewStringBuilder = New StringBuilder
End Function
```

Listing 15 Function to Create an Object

If you have an Object that needs an argument list, provide the list to the Factory Function, and thence to the requisite startup Methods.

Put this Function into Support.accde, or in a Module in which you collect all your Factories. Make another backup copy of Support.accdb and Save & Publish it as an ACCDE.

Remember to include the Module as a Reference to your project.

Using the Object Factory

The Usual Object
The usual way to make an Object looks like this:

```
Dim sb As StringBuilder
Set sb = New StringBuilder

'  USE sb

Set sb = Nothing
```

Listing 16 The Usual way to make an Object

The Factory Object
The way to make an Object using the Factory
looks like this:

```
Dim sb As StringBuilder
Set sb = NewStringBuilder

'  USE sb

Set sb = Nothing
```

Listing 17 The Factory-made Object

The only difference is that now we are calling our
Factory Function to produce the Object. It might
be more obvious what we're doing if we change
the name of our Function to something like Cre-
ateStringBuilder, or FactoryStringBuilder(?).

Preserving and reusing your work
From here, follow the same process as archiving
Modules. Include Factory modules, and Class
modules in Support.accdb as shown in Commandment IX.

Note that to use Modules and Classes in other apps of the Microsoft Office suite, you'll need to make your support code compatible with the other apps. Access database modules aren't compatible with Word, say, so you'll need to structure your code differently.

APPENDIXES

Appendix A – VBA from Zero

VBA Code

The human brain has two lobes. They say that one lobe processes text, while the other processes images and visual patterns. Code is text, so when we're coding, we're writing text, and we're using half our brain.

One way to double our effectiveness is to get the visual pattern lobe involved in our coding. We do this by limiting the number of different forms of code statements. That is, when we see a textual pattern on a page or on a screen, the visual processor of the brain recognizes the shape of the code, and the textual processor of the brain recognizes the details.

BASIC was a small language to start with, and using only a bit of VBA is consistent with that original aim. VBA is a smorgasbord; one need not eat everything to enjoy the experience.

Projects

Projects are the organizing entity that holds Modules, and References to external code libraries.

Modules

Modules are the outermost code containers. Everything else is within them.

Procedures

Procedures are a named sequence of statements executed as a unit. They exist in the forms of

Functions and Subs. Functions explicitly return a value to the code that calls it, whereas Subs don't.

The scheme for each is shown in the following table. These are amplified versions of diagrams in the VBA help file. Interpret this code as follows:

- [content] within brackets is optional.

- The vertical bar "|" says "choose one of the expressions I separate"

Functions & Subs

[Public | Private] Function *name* [**(** *arglist***)**] [**As** *type*]
    [*Setup statements*]
    =============
    [*statements*]
    [*name* **=** *expression*]
    [**GoTo** *exitProcessing*]
    [*statements*]
    [*name* **=** *expression*]
    =============
exitProcessing:
    [*statements*]
errorExit:
    [*statements*]
End Function

Functions & Subs (cont'd)

[**Private** | **Public**] **Sub** *name* [(*arglist*)]
  [*Setup statements*]
  =============
  [*statements*]
  [**GoTo** e*xitprocessing*]
  [*statements*]
  =============
exitProcessing:
  [*statements*]
errorExit:
  [*statements*]
End Sub

Statements

Statements are the next inner layer, contained by Procedures. VBA has more than seventy kinds of statements in which to write code. It is rare that anyone would use all seventy in a single calculation, and there are many that won't be used in a lifetime.

Begin your discovery of statements and how to write them by searching the VBA help for "Writing Visual Basic Statements".

Statements are organized in two ways

- The Five Code Constructs

- Statements

The Five Code Constructs

Code constructs are statements that contain other statements. Each has multiple parts, and

different ways of using them. They control the
flow of program execution.

Because there are so many constructs, it's important that we limit which ones we even look at.

The following table contains constructs that are
amplified from those shown in VBA help. These
five are the ones you'll use. Stick with these and
avoid variants.

Choosing

Constructs: Choosing	
Construct	**Notes**

If *condition* **Then**
    [*statements*]
    ...
[**ElseIf** *condition-n* **Then**
    [*elseifstatements*]]
    ...
[**Else**
    [*elsestatements*]]
End If
	Any of the statement clauses is optional. If omitted, nothing happens.

Select Case *testexpression*
    [**Case** *expressionlist-n*
        [*statements-n*]]
        ...
    [**Case Else**
        [*elsestatements*]]
End Select
	Any of the statement clauses is optional. If omitted, nothing happens.

The proper way to write an If statement is to always use the three-line pattern of Listing 18, instead of the one-line pattern of Listing 19 (which should be treated as a curse)

```
If condition Then
        ' do something
End If
```

Listing 18 Proper If statement

```
If condition Then dosomething
```

Listing 19 One-line If statement

condition is an expression that evaluates to a Boolean value of True or False. This can be as simple as

```
count > 0
```

a calculation that compares *count* with 0. The calculation result is True if *count* is greater than 0, and False if *count* is less than or equal to 0.

The code between the If and the End If is indented to show that it is controlled by the If statement. The brain's pattern lobe (left or right depending on who you are) gets used to seeing this pattern, and it will alert us when the statement is the wrong shape. The wrong shape usually indicates something is fishy.

The three-line shape increases coding speed, too. You will often need to modify the construct to control more than one statement by adding lines that do something more. The indented pictorial structure of the text remains the same. The End If is already in place, so you don't have to add it along with the additional statements.

When *condition* is complicated, write it in a Boolean function procedure. Call the function as part of the If statement.

```
If TheseConditions(a,b,c) Then
   '  do something
End If
```

Listing 20 If condition as a function

And note that we write

```
If  Condition Then
```

rather than

```
If  Condition = True Then
```

What if the number of *do something* statements controlled by the If becomes large, as in Listing 21?

```
If TheseConditions(a, b, c) Then
   '   Many statement calculations
   stmt1
   stmt2
   ...
   stmt n
End If
```

Listing 21 If controlling many statements

The pattern starts to disappear. The 'Many statement comment is a clue as to how we should write this code: use the comment as the name of a procedure, and move those many statements into the procedure as in Listing 22

```
If (TheseConditions(a, b, c)) Then
    result = ManyStatements
End If
```

Listing 22 If with two functions

Thus, the text pattern is preserved, and points toward the idea of Stepwise Refinement, a method invented in 1971 by Niklaus Wirth. When thinking about, and writing, code, use comments as the names of calculations. After the calculation idea is developed, replace the comments with the names of procedures that will do the calculations.

Note that in the statement

```
result = ManyStatements
```

the equals sign is used to assign the result of the calculation to the variable named *result*. VBA also uses the '=' in Boolean statements to test the equality of two expressions. Thus, you may occasionally run across (or write) statements like

```
result = a = b
```

which reads from right to left! It compares a to b and assigns the truth of that comparison to result. It may be preferable to put the a = b into a Function of its own. Or at least, surround it: (a = b)

Choosing between two or more alternatives will follow the similar pattern, and here it's worthwhile to insert some blank lines, too:

```
If (TheseConditions(a, b, c)) Then
   result = ManyStatements

ElseIf (ThoseConditions(a, b, d)) Then
   result = SomeOtherCalculations

Else
   result = DefaultCalculations

End If
```

Listing 23 If-ElseIf-Else pattern

The white-space accentuates the pattern and makes for easier reading.

One final note about If Else:
Write the statement such that the shortest do something comes first, and the longest is in the Else. To do this, you may have to invert the logical sense of the If, and write

```
If Not Condition Then
   '   fewer statements
Else
   '   more statements
   '   etc.
End If
```

Listing 24 If with reversed condition

Select Case

Constructs: Choosing	
Construct	**Notes**

Select Case *testexpression*
[**Case** *expressionlist-n*
  [*statements-n*]]
  ...
  [**Case Else**
    [*elsestatements*]]
End Select
	Any of the state-
	ment clauses is
	optional. If omit-
	ted, nothing hap-
	pens.

This construct embodies a method of choosing a
program option when there are many cases from
which to choose. Because there are many cases,
however, it's easy to gum up the works and lose
track of what the calculation is supposed to be
doing. Therefore, for each case involved, use at
most 2 or 3 lines to encapsulate the choice. Better
of course is a 1-line call to a procedure whose
name reflects the calculation. Such minimization
makes it easy to test each calculation sepa-
rately(!).

Iterating

Iteration statements are at the heart of VBA computing. The machine does the tedious work while we watch. A few guidelines minimize their complexity:

- Loops must end.

- Termination is determined at the top of a loop only.

- A procedure contains at most one loop.

- If a calculation "requires" loop nesting, put the inner loop in a procedure*.

Use three, not eight

There are at least eight iteration statements available in VBA. Use these three, only:

- For...Next

- For Each...Next

- Do While...Loop

---

* The exceptions to this guideline are calculations involving matrices and multiply subscripted arrays.

For...Next Statement

For *counter* = *start* **To** *end* [**Step** *step*]
  [*statements*]
  [GoTo continue]
  [*statements*]
  [Exit For]
  [*statements*]
continue:
  Next [*counter*]
	GoTo continue allows calculations to resume with the next *counter* step.
	
	Exit For jumps out of the loop to the statement following **Next**

Figure 20 For...Next schematic

Initialization for the For...Next statement is **explicit**. It starts a counter at some start value, and executes the statements between the For and the Next. When execution meets the Next [counter] statement, counter is bumped by the value of step, and control transfers back to the top of the loop for the test counter = end.

Notes

All of the statement components in brackets are optional.

For neatness, include the optional counter with the Next.

If unspecified, the default value of step is 1.

To iterate backwards, specify step as a negative number.

The Exit For is yet another GoTo in disguise. The jump is out of the loop to the statement immediately following the Next.

Example

```
'  iterating up
'
Dim i As Long
For i = 1 To 3
    Debug.Print i
Next i

'  iterating down
'
For i = 3 To 1 Step -1
    Debug.Print i
Next i
```

Listing 25 For...Next iteration

Possible problems

The For statement requires counting something, which may have no relation to the calculation you're performing, and then you have to use a trick to get the code to do what you want. In this case, it's better to use the Do While, write the loop control that relates to the problem, and avoid trickery.

Nowhere does VBA limit what you can do with this code, nor does it say what data type counter must be. It should be an integral type, as shown in Listing 25, but here's a possible BAD PRACTICE:

```
Dim x As Double
For x = 1 To 2 Step 0.3
   Debug.Print x
   x = x - 0.01
Next x
```
Listing 26 BAD PRACTICE For... Next loop

The output from this little loop is

```
1
1.29
1.58
1.87
```

Well, OK, maybe that's what you meant to do. But what if the loop is written this way

```
Dim x As Double
Dim y As Double
y = 0.3
For x = 1 To 2 Step 0.3
   Debug.Print x
   x = x - y
Next x
```
Listing 27 Even WORSE BAD PRACTICE For... Next loop

The output from x is

1
1
1
1
1
… forever

It's what's called an infinite loop. The sins committed here are two-fold:

- The loop counter is not an integral data type;

- The value of the loop counter is modified inside the loop.

Avoid both of these problems by using the Do While…Loop construct.

For Each...Next Statement

For Each *element* **In** *group*
  [*statements*]
  [**GoTo continue**]
  [*statements*]
  [**Exit For**]
  [*statements*]
continue:
  Next [*element*]
	Each *element* in *group* is visited, subject to the alterations
	
	GoTo continue allows calculations to resume with the next *element* in the *group*.
	
	Exit For jumps out of the loop to the statement following **Next**

Figure 21 For Each...Next schematic

This code structure supports iteration over objects in a collection.

Notes

- Initialization for the For Each...Next statement is **im**plicit.

- The group in this iteration is a collection of objects, and the For Each statement sets each element as a pointer to each object, and cleans up each object afterwards

- The statements operate on each element of a group in turn.

- The loop "knows" how many elements are in the group, so it knows when to terminate.

- Include the optional element of the collection with the Next

- The Exit For is yet another cloaked GoTo. Executing the statement transfers the execution point to the statement immediately following the Next element statement.

- The For Each...Next statement is what is known as "syntactic sugar". It conceals much management dealing with the instantiation of objects and their cleanup.

Example

Examine the tables in a database:

```
Dim tdef As TableDef
For Each tdef In CurrentDb.TableDefs
    Debug.Print tdef.Name
Next tdef
```

Listing 28 Example For Each...Next iteration

Do While...Loop Statement

Do While *condition*
    [*statements*]
    [**GoTo continue**]
    [*statements*]
    [**Exit Do**]
    [*statements*]
continue:
    [*statements*]
Loop
	Somewhere in the loop, "condition" must change.
	
	GoTo continue calculations resume with the next iteration in sequence.
	
	Exit Do jumps to the statement following **Loop**

Figure 22 Do While__Loop schematic

Use this statement for flexible looping. You are responsible for explicit loop control.

Notes

All of the statement components in brackets are optional.

The Exit Do is yet another GoTo in disguise. The jump is out of the loop to the statement immediately following the Loop. Do not use these indiscriminately.

condition may be any expression that evaluates to True or False. Often this is a call to a Boolean Function.

The Do While is especially good for the case when nothing needs to be done, which is why the test at the top of the loop is preferable.

Example

Consider using a Recordset to access data in a table. You can use VBA to move through a table using the RBAR method: Row By Agonizing Row. Really, if you're accessing data, you're usually better off using SQL queries. Nonetheless, the capability exists in VBA, and you might have to use it. Supposing such a need, we have this structure:

```
'  initialize
Dim rst As Recordset
Set rst = CurrentDb.OpenRecordset ("QueryOrTable", _
    dbOpenDynaset)

Do While Not rst.EOF
'==============================
      '  deal with current recordset
    rst.MoveNext   '  reinit
'==============================
Loop

rst.Close
Set rst = Nothing
```

Listing 29 Iterating over a Recordset

The code to deal with each row of the table is placed between the '==... comment sandwich. Any other termination condition can be set inside the loop, but tested only on the While line. Suppose we only want to deal with the first 10 rows of a table. Code to reflect this requirement might look like this

```
Dim rowno As Long:   rowno = 0
Do While (Not rst.EOF) And (rowno < 10)
'===============================
   '  deal with current row
   Debug.Print rst!SSN
   rowno = rowno + 1
   etc.
'===============================
Loop
```

Listing 30 Augmenting a While termination condition

Anathema: Do NOT to use these five:

Do...Loop Statement 2

Do Until *condition*]
   [*statements*]
   [**Exit Do**]
   [*statements*]
Loop

Do...Loop Statements 3 & 4

Do
   [*statements*]
   [**Exit Do**]
   [*statements*]
Loop [{While | Until} *condition*]

While...Wend Statement

While condition
   [statements]
Wend

If...Goto statement

TopOfLoop:
If *condition* **Then**
   [*statements*]
   [**GoTo** *BottomOfLoop*]
   [*statements*]
   [**GoTo** *OutOfLoop*]
   [statements]
BottomOfLoop:
   [statements]
End If
OutOfLoop:

They are included here so you can recognize
them if you run across them.

Indenting your code

While it is possible to write VBA flush left, VCA allows you to indent your code properly. We spoke of visual code patterns earlier, and code indentation is responsible for pattern formation and recognition. If your inherited database code is not indented, don't knock yourself out indenting by hand (Commandment III) – use an on-line indenter. Two that are useful:

> http://www.vbindent.com/?indent

and

> https://www.automateexcel.com/
> vba-code-indenter/#

Neither are perfect, but they will save you a ton of work.

Statements

Now let's look at the innermost of the Matryoshka dolls, the VBA *statement*.

The following table lists the plain statements
newbies need to study in the Help file. Of course,
you may use any statement, even if you don't
know what you're doing, but there is a minimum
of statements needed to begin trusted coding.

Your reading assignment is to thoroughly read
the VBA Help file re the following **Statements
Needed for Trusted Code** Table.

Statements Needed for Trusted Code	
Statement	Notes
Assignment	Cf. "Writing assignment state-ments" in the Help file.
Dim	Declares variables and allocates storage space.
GoTo *linelabel*	Branches unconditionally to the specified labeled line within a pro-cedure.
On Error	Enables an error handling routine in a procedure
Private	Declare variables and procedures to be available only to the Module in which they are declared
Public	Variables and procedures declared Public are available to all proce-dures in all Modules
Resume [*linelabel*]	A GoTo statement only available in an error-handler
Stop	Suspends execution. Use during development only.
Exit Function	Immediately leave the current Function.
Exit Sub	Immediately leave the current Sub

The **Module level statements** table lists the declarations you MUST include at the top of every one of your Modules. No exceptions.

Module level statements	
Statement	Notes
Option Compare Database	Used at module level to declare the default comparison method to use when string data is compared. Required in all Modules. Provided by the VBE.
Option Explicit	Used at module level to force explicit declaration of all variables in that module. Required in all Modules.

Appendix B – VCA productions

Each of the VBA Code Assistant (VCA) productions is detailed below, with the **Name** and **Description** textboxes filled as shown in Figure 23 to allow easy recognition in the code. Obviously, avoid the use of *Name*, and make your Description useful.

Figure 23 Fields set for examples

The labels and content of the textboxes will change depending on the Code Type.

Accessibility affects *Func*, *Sub*, and *RstFunc* only.

Func

A standard function plus a Private Sub for testing.
Likely modifications include:

- Calculations in the comment sandwich.
- Data type of returned value (and result).

```
'
Private Function Name() As Boolean
'  Purpose: Name - Information from the Description Textbox
    On Error GoTo errorExit
    Dim result As Boolean
    result = False
    '==============================

    '==============================
exitProcessing:
    On Error Resume Next
    Name = result
    Exit Function

errorExit:
    Debug.Print Err.Description
    Stop
    Resume exitprocessing
    Resume

End Function   '  Name
```

```
Private Sub XName
    Dim result as Boolean
    result = Name
End Sub   '  XName
```

Sub

A standard Sub plus a test driver.

Likely modifications include:

- Calculations in the comment sandwich.

```
'

Private Sub Name()
'  Purpose: Name - Information from the Description
Textbox
    On Error GoTo errorExit
    '===============================

    '===============================
exitProcessing:
    On Error Resume Next
    Exit Sub

errorExit:
    Debug.Print Err.Description
    Stop
    Resume exitprocessing
    Resume

End Sub   '   Name
```

```
Private Sub XName
    Name
End Sub   '   XName
```

RstFunc

A function that opens a Recordset on either a table or a query, and provides access to each record in the Recordset. This function is a last resort, when you can't figure out how to do the calculation with SQL.

Likely modifications include:

- Truth of the returned value result.
- Calculations in the comment sandwich. Because the function may iterate over all the records of a recordset, the Name of this function should be something like FooAllTheBars. The calculation in the comment sandwich should then be a call to a Func or Sub with a name like FooASingleBar(rst).

First, the test driver:

```
Private Sub XName
    Dim result as Boolean
    result = Name
End Sub  '  XName
```

And then, the function, which contains the *continue:* label at the bottom of the loop. Sometimes you need a way to jump to the next iteration, rather than exit the Do, and this is a handy tag to have. If you don't need it, delete it.

```
Private Function Name() As Boolean
'  Purpose: Name - Information from the Description Textbox
   On Error GoTo errorExit
   Dim result As Boolean
   result = False
   '===============================

   Dim db As DAO.Database
   Set db = CurrentDb
   Dim rst As Recordset
   Set rst = CurrentDb.OpenRecordset("QueryOrTable", _
          dbOpenDynaset)

   Do While Not rst.EOF

continue:
      rst.MoveNext
Loop

   rst.Close
   Set rst = Nothing
   '===============================
exitProcessing:
   On Error Resume Next
   Name = result
   Exit Function

errorExit:
   Debug.Print Err.Description
   Stop
   Resume exitprocessing
   Resume

End Function   '   Name
```

Prop

A property of a class, with *m_Name* as the name of the property field. The "m_" prefix is a somewhat classical practice pun intended, hence the use of the underscore.

Likely modifications include

- Moving the field to the top of the class.
- Commenting out either the Get or the Let function
- Changing the property data type. Note that if it's possible for a property to be Null, the stored type must be a Variant.

```
Private m_Name as Variant

Public Property Get Name() As Variant
    Name = m_Name
End Property
```

```
Public Property Let Name(ByVal vNewValue As Variant)
    m_Name = vNewValue
End Property
```

Object

It is desirable to clean up after using VBA classes, but I get tired of having to type this repetitive code. In the VCA, enter the Object name and Class name in the appropriate textboxes.

The first line produced declares the name of the object of the class.

The second line "news it up", or makes an object of the class.

The third line disposes of the object.

Likely modifications:

- Move the third line to the exit point of the procedure that creates it.

```
Dim myObject as ObjectTextBox contents
Set myObject = New ClassName
set myObject = Nothing
```

Program

VCA generates more than 100 lines of code comprising Public Sub Name, and Private procedures Init, Run, and Fini along with test procedures for each. Trace is turned on automatically.

Modifications as needed.

```
'
Public Sub Name()
'  Purpose: Name - Information from the Description
Textbox
    On Error GoTo errorExit
    Enter "Name"   '  Tracing
    Dim result as Boolean
'=====================================
    result = Init

    If (result) Then
       result = Run
    End If

    result = Fini(result)
    '==============================
exitProcessing:
    On Error Resume Next
    Leave "Name"
    Exit Sub

errorExit:
    Debug.Print Err.Description
    Stop
    Resume exitprocessing
    Resume

End Sub
```

```
Private Sub XName
   Name
End Sub
```

'

```
Private Function Init(result as Boolean) as Boolean
'  Purpose: Init - initializations
   On Error GoTo errorExit
   Enter "Init"    '  Tracing
   '================================

   '================================
exitProcessing:
   On Error Resume Next
   Init = result
   Leave "Init"
   Exit Function

errorExit:
   Debug.Print Err.Description
   Stop
   Resume exitprocessing
   Resume

End Function
```

```
Private Sub XInit
   Dim result as Boolean
   result = Init(result)
End Sub
```

```
'

Private Function Run(result as Boolean) as Boolean
'  Purpose: Run - main calculations
   On Error GoTo errorExit
   Enter "Run"    '  Tracing
   '===============================


   '===============================
exitProcessing:
   On Error Resume Next
   Run = result
   Leave "Run"
   Exit Function


errorExit:
   Debug.Print Err.Description
   Stop
   Resume exitprocessing
   Resume

End Function
```

```
Private Sub XRun
   Dim result as Boolean
   result = Run
End Sub
```

```
'

Private Function Fini(result as Boolean) as Boolean
' Purpose: Fini - clean up
    On Error GoTo errorExit
    Enter "Fini"   ' Tracing
    '================================
    If result Then
        Debug.Print "Success"
    Else
        Debug.Print "Failure"
    End If
    '================================
exitProcessing:
    On Error Resume Next
    Fini = result
    Leave "Fini"
    Exit Function

errorExit:
    Debug.Print Err.Description
    Stop
    Resume exitprocessing
    Resume

End Function
```

```
Private Sub XFini
    Dim result as Boolean
    result = Fini(result)
End Sub
```

Err Handler

A Simple or Detailed error handler is generated
to accept input from your procedure error traps.

Simple

Perhaps too simple. At least add a Stop and De-
bug.Print Procname

```
'
Private Sub ErrorHandler( procName as String )
'   Purpose: ErrorHandler - Simple Error Handler
    '================================


    '================================
End Sub
```

Detailed

Use this error handler when you want to store
the information somewhere, such as in a table.

- *err* is the error object; examine its properties to see what's important
- *procName* is the procedure in which the
  error occurred
- *lno* is the line number at which the error
  occurred. Use MZTools to turn line num-
  bering on and off

'

```
Private Sub ErrorReport( err as Object, _
    procName as String, lno as Long )
'  Purpose: ErrorReport - Detailed Error Handler
    '================================

    '================================
End Sub
```

If Else

A standard "if else" construct. The label for the Name Textbox changes to 'IF Condition'.

Likely modifications:

- Change Name to the desired expression.
- In the lines immediately following the *If*, write the code to be executed if the test is true. Should you want to "do nothing", you can omit writing any statements – the statement still works properly.
- In the lines immediately following the *Else*, write the code to be executed if the test is false. If there is no *Else* part to do, write nothing.

```
If IFCondition Then


Else
End If
```

- On the other hand, if you want to "do nothing", it sometimes makes code clearer to insert a comment in the idle part of the construct.

```
If IFCondition Then
    …some calculation
Else
    '  do nothing
End If
```

If ElseIf Else

A standard "if elseif else" construct. When you need more ElseIfs, use the ElseIf radio button.

When the number of ElseIfs gets "large", consider using the Select Case statement.

Selecting the "If ElseIf Else" VCA radio button changes the textbox labels to "IF Condition" and "ELSE IF Condition". Enter your conditions on the VCA form.

Likely modifications:

- Fill in the code to be executed per the applicable truth.
- Use or discard the final just-in-case "Else"

```
If IFCondition Then


Elself ELSEIFCondition Then
   '   ⇐ more code here
Else
End If
```

ElseIf

A standard ElseIf clause to an If statement. This is included in the tool for completeness, but most of the time, it's easier to simply type the few characters required.

Likely modifications:

- Replace IFCondition with the appropriate Boolean expression.

ElseIf IFCondition Then

End If

Select Case

Use this construct when you need to choose among multiple possibilities, as an alternative to a chain of "If-Else If-etc." statements. Each of the cases is separate. When the code for a Case is finished, execution resumes after the End Select statement.

Because these statements can potentially have many lines, it is best to limit each "Case: Action" construct to a single line. This is best achieved by limiting Action to a single Function or Sub call.

Selecting "Select Case" changes the labels on VCA as shown in

Figure 24

Figure 24 Label changes on VCA form for Select Case

The SELECT variable textbox is used to specify the variable controlling the Select. Each "word" in the Description textbox is used as a Case value. If you are selecting on strings, enter a double quote (") as the first character. As shown in

Figure 24, the code produced is

```
Select Case Name

    Case "Information"
        Debug.Print "Information"

    Case "from"
        Debug.Print "from"
        '    etc.

    Case "the"
        Debug.Print "the"

    Case "Description"
        Debug.Print "Description"

    Case "textbox"
        Debug.Print "textbox"

    Case Else

End Select
```

Likely modifications:

- Code in the "Case Else" option might direct to an error handler.

For...Next

Iterate over a collection of values, often in an array.

Note that VCA inserts a labeled 'continue:' statement immediately preceding the loop terminator. This is for those situations when you need to stop messing with the current item and move on to the next one in sequence.

To jump out of the loop entirely, use the VBA statement "Exit For", which takes you to the statement immediately following the "Next".

Likely modifications:

- Change the iteration variable from *i* to something else.
- The upper bound of *1* to the actual upper bound of the array. The VBA standard *UBound* function may be helpful.
- Optionally remove the "continue:" label.

```
Dim i As Long
For i = 1 To 1


continue:
  Next i
```

Reverse iteration from high to low requires adding the *step* clause, with a negative increment for *i*.

For Each...Next

Iteration over a collection of objects, often a VBA collection.

Clicking this radio button changes the VCA form as shown in Figure 25

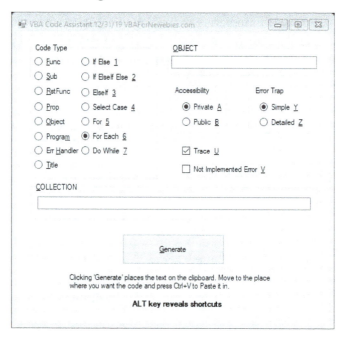

Figure 25 VCA Form with 'For Each' selected

Note that VCA inserts a labeled "continue:" statement immediately preceding the loop terminator. This is for those situations when you need to stop messing with the current object and move on to the next one in sequence. To exit the loop entirely, use the VBA statement "Exit For", which takes you to the statement immediately following "Next".

```
For Each tdef In TableDefs
```

```
continue:
    Next tdef
    Set tdef = Nothing
```

VCA adds the statement to set the loop Object to Nothing because VBA doesn't always discard that variable as it is supposed to. When these Objects hang around, they interfere with proper Access shut-down.

Do While...Loop

Do While...Loop iterates as long as *Condition* is true. It is possible that the loop never executes, or never terminates.

Unless you're deliberately writing an infinite loop, some statement within the loop must change the value of *Condition*.

Note that VCA inserts a labeled 'continue:' statement immediately preceding the loop terminator. This is for those situations when you need to stop messing with the current thing and move on to the next one in sequence. To exit the loop entirely, use the VBA statement "Exit Do", which takes you to the statement immediately following "Loop".

```
Do While Condition

continue:
    Loop
```

Error Trap

We have two options for the error trap: Simple and Detailed.

The simplest really *is* an error trap. This trap immediately turns subsequent action over to the developer.

```
errorExit:
   Debug.Print Err.Description
   Stop
   Resume exitprocessing
   Resume
```

The more elaborate error handler is labeled "Detailed". The code produced is

```
errorExit:
   ErrorReport Err, "Name", Erl
   Resume exitprocessing
   Resume
```

This requires you to have a separate public procedure named *ErrorReport* somewhere in your project. You might use this error handler if you want to store error occurrences in a table. It might look something like

```
'

Public Sub ErrorReport(err as Object, _
      procName as String, lno as Long )
'  Purpose: ErrorReport – and Handler
      '================================

      '================================
End Sub
```

Trace option

The Trace checkbox adds code at the entry and exit points of a procedure. It requires the *Trace* module be part of the application code. Cf. Appendix C for the full code of *Trace*.

Checking the Trace option changes the Function production to

```
Private Function Name() As Boolean
'  Purpose: Name - Description
    On Error GoTo errorExit
    Enter "Name"   '  Tracing
    Dim result As Boolean
    result = False
    '===============================


    '===============================
exitProcessing:
    On Error Resume Next
    Name = result
    Leave "Name"
    Exit Function

errorExit:
    Debug.Print Err.Description
    Stop
    Resume exitprocessing
    Resume

End Function
```

```
Private Sub XName
    Dim result as Boolean
    result = Name
End Sub
```

Not Implemented Error

During some development projects, the aim is to show as much progress as possible. This can mean adding procedures, but not developing the contents thereof. This option allows the code to be compiled, but when it comes to testing, procedures that have no code raise an error.

Checking the Not Implemented Error option changes the Func production to

```
'
Private Function Name() As Boolean
'  Purpose: Name - Description
   On Error GoTo errorExit
   Dim result As Boolean
   result = False
   '==============================
   Err.Raise vbObjectError + 513,, _
      "Name NOT IMPLEMENTED"
   '==============================
exitProcessing:
   On Error Resume Next
   Name = result
   Exit Function


errorExit:
   Debug.Print Err.Description
   Stop
   Resume exitprocessing
   Resume


End Function
```

Title

This radiobutton provides a 40-character comment line to put a "title" in your code, like this

```
'======================================
'               Name
```

in which "Name" is centered within the 40 columns.

Appendix C – The Trace Module

Commandment VI showed a fundamental Trace Module. Consider now, the following extensions.

Trace.Reset

A Reset statement would be useful as the first statement in a program that uses Trace. The VBE is *supposed* to set everything to 0 when a program is restarted, but that is not always the case. The procedure name 'Reset' is likely to be a name that could easily appear in other modules. Specifying the Module name ensures that we are calling the Reset procedure in the Trace Module:

Trace.Reset

On the other hand, I could have named the procedure TraceReset, like the following On / Off procedures.

TraceOn

to turn the tracing on (the default).

TraceOff

to turn it off.

IsTraceOn

Returns True if the current Trace state is On.

The On and Off functions are useful when a procedure is called many times (in a loop, say) and you don't need to hear from the procedure inside the loop that's being called so often. It's a tossup to turn Trace off, or comment out the calls to Enter and Leave.

Caveats
Calls to Trace are most easily inserted when your procedures are generated by a tool.

The interface
As Trace users, all we need to interact with is the interface to the procedures shown in Listing 31. The procedures are listed in the order of use.

```
Public Sub Enter(procName As String)

Public Sub Leave(procName As String)

Public Sub Reset()

Public Sub TraceOn()

Public Sub TraceOff()

Public Function IsTraceOn() as Boolean
```
Listing 31 Trace Interface

We'll need an internal variable to keep track of *On* and *Off*.

```
Private m_Indent As Long
Private m_isOff   As Boolean
```
Listing 32 Internal Trace variables

Why m_isOff rather than m_isOn?. I usually like to accentuate the positive, but the default state of a VBA Boolean variable is *False*. Before execution starts, VBA (is supposed to) initialize all Boolean variables to *False*. We want the default state of Trace to be On. Therefore, at startup, any Boolean variable we use will be set to False. The simple way to have the startup state of Trace to be On is to let VBA set Off to False.

Enter

An outline for this procedure is shown in Listing 33

```
Public Sub Enter(procName As String)
    If Trace is on Then
        Print procname indented
        IncreaseIndent
    End If
End Sub
```

Listing 33 Outline of *Enter*

The test "Trace is on" can be replaced by our function *IsTraceOn*. We put this code into a Function because the logic is a little convoluted, and we don't want to have to go through the reversal thinking of On/Off; we just want the answer.

When it comes to the "Print" statement, we can replace that with

```
Debug.Print Space(m_Indent) & "Enter " & procName
```

186 | A p p e n d i x   C   –   T h e   T r a c e
M o d u l e

Space() is a built-in VBA function that returns a
String of blank characters. m_Indent starts out as
0, so the first call to Enter will have an indent of 0.

The "&" characters mean "String concatenation",
so the string that will be output will look like

(perhaps spaces)Enter procname

After our refinements, Enter winds up as this procedure

```
Public Sub Enter(procNam As String)
    If IsTraceOn Then
        Debug.Print Space(m_Indent) & "Enter " & procNam
        IncreaseIndent
    End If
End Sub
```

Listing 34 Enter complete

Leave

Leave will be the mirror image of Enter, and it
will look like this

```
Public Sub Leave(procNam As String)
    If IsTraceOn Then
        DecreaseIndent
        Debug.Print Space(m_Indent) & "Leave " & procNam
    End If
End Sub
```

Listing 35 Leave, complete

IncreaseIndent

Of course, we need to provide some code to re-place the lines IncreaseIndent and DecreaseIn-dent. The simplest way to do that is to write two procedures that are private to the Trace Module.

IncreaseIndent needs to increase the indent, and guard against pushing things out the window if the indent gets "too large". Therefore, we'll set a constant

```
Const MAXINDENT As Long = 10
```

at the top of the file, and use that as a control on indenting. It's a lot easier to read code that *describes* what "10" is, rather than to sprinkle magic numbers through a Module. Constants are Private by default.

After thinking this through, IncreaseIndent should: increase the indent by 1, but not exceed MAXINDENT. Our code looks like this

```
Private Sub IncreaseIndent()
    m_Indent = Min(m_Indent + 1, MAXINDENT)
End Sub
```

Listing 36 IncreaseIndent complete

Min is a function that returns the minimum of two Longs, so the one statement in this procedure says "Add 1 to m_Indent, and compare that to MAXINDENT. Return the minimum of those two values, and set m_Indent to that value. While SQL

has a Min function, VBA doesn't! So we'll write
that in a moment.

DecreaseIndent

DecreaseIndent will be the mirror image of IncreaseIndent. This time, we don't want to run off
the window to the left, so the most DecreaseIndent can decrease to is 0.

With this in mind, the code looks like this

```
Private Sub DecreaseIndent()
    m_Indent = Max(m_Indent - 1, 0)
End Sub
```

Listing 37 IncreaseIndent complete

Max is a function that returns the maximum of
two Longs. VBA doesn't provide it, either, so we'll
write Min and Max now.

Min & Max

Min and Max are two functions that wrap If...Else
statements. Here are both of them.

```
Private Function Min(a As Long, b As Long) As Long
   If a <= b Then
      Min = a
   Else
      Min = b
   End If
End Function
```

```
Private Function Max(a As Long, b As Long) _
      As Long
   If a >= b Then
      Max = a
   Else
      Max = b
   End If
End Function
```

Listing 38 Min and Max functions

Trace state

The procedures that modify and reveal the state
of tracing are simple interfaces to the m_isOff internal variable.

```
Public Sub TraceOn()
   m_isOff = False
End Sub
```

```
Public Sub TraceOff()
   m_isOff = True
End Sub
```

```
Public Function IsTraceOn() as Boolean
   IsTraceOn = Not m_isOff
End Function
```

Listing 39 Procedures monitoring Trace state

One scenario for the use of these three procedures is a case where a tested procedure is in a loop executed many times.

```
Private Function StillTesting() As Boolean
   '  ...
   Do While n < 1000000
   '================================
      result = testedFunction(n)
      TraceOff
   '================================
   Loop
   TraceOn
   '  ...
End Function
```

Listing 40 When to turn off Trace

In this code, the call to *testedFunction* is printed once rather than a million times. The call to

TraceOn must be before the Exit, else the rest of the trace will be lost.

Why no error handling in this Module!?

There is no need for error code. All the data is interior to the Module, and the only way to access it is through the interface, which controls the values to a set of known values.

Where to put this code?

Trace is a useful extension to the VBE, but you don't want to write it more than once. It should be stored somewhere outside the current working database, so you can use it on more than one project. We use an Access database named 'Support.accde'. The only things in our Support database are Modules. Cf. Commandment XI. Thou shalt archive Modules.

Code

The entire *Trace* Module is below. The Public routines, those available to the outside world, are in boldface; the rest of the code is support for those four procedures.

You can turn the trace on and off using the TraceOn and TraceOff Subs, respectively. You're on your own to keep them balanced.

This Module looks like a Class, but it's not. If you need more than one Trace going on at the same time, you will need to make this a Class, and instantiate each one. The tradeoff here is that as a Module, you can Enter and Exit single procedures without having to initiate Trace; VBA will do it for you.

The *Min* and *Max* functions are useful in their own right; you might consider including them in a general utility Module. Change the data type of the arguments and the functions to *Variant* so you can use them with all types, including *Dates* and *Strings*. Make sure you don't compare apples to oranges.

```
Option Compare Database
Option Explicit

Const MAXINDENT As Integer = 10

Private m_Indent    As Integer
Private m_isOff     As Boolean

Public Sub Enter(procName As String)
  If (Not m_isOff) Then
  Debug.Print Space(m_Indent) & _
    "Enter " & procName
    IncreaseIndent
  End If
End Sub

Public Sub Leave(procName As String)
  If (Not m_isOff) Then
    DecreaseIndent
  Debug.Print Space(m_Indent) & _
    "Leave " & procName
  End If
End Sub

Public Sub TraceOn()
  m_isOff = False
End Sub

Public Sub TraceOff()
  m_isOff = True
End Sub
```

```
Private Sub IncreaseIndent()
   m_Indent = Min(m_Indent + 1, MAXINDENT)
End Sub
```

```
Private Function Min(a As Integer, b As Integer) _
As Integer
   If a < b Then
      Min = a
   Else
      Min = b
   End If
End Function
```

```
Private Sub DecreaseIndent()
   m_Indent = Max(m_Indent - 1, 0)
End Sub
```

```
Private Function Max(a As Integer, b As Integer) _
As Integer
   If a > b Then
      Max = a
   Else
      Max = b
   End If
End Function
```

Possible Extensions

Timing

Even further inside the Module, with limited exposure to the outside world, we can call the system clock and record the times of Enter and Leave. This is an easy way to start measuring your program's performance.

Level vs Indent

An alternative representation of the call structure can be traced with an integer variable "level". Now, rather than a listing in the Immediate window, each procedure call can be stored in a table for later analysis.

Appendix D - A Big Example

In this appendix, we present an app that we used during the production of this book, along with the other tools Word makes available. It offers us the chance to include not only references to the VBA commandments, but citations of Good Practice as we encounter them in the development effort.

The Problem

Microsoft Word shows some statistics about documents. Still, there are a few things Word doesn't do. We'd like:

- counts of each word, so we get an idea of the vocabulary of a text;
- the opportunity to consider simple substitutes for rare words;
- to ensure that the text is as simple as possible, while retaining a flavor of salt.
- to replace repetitive phrases with variations, so the writing isn't stale.

One way to satisfy these desires is with an app that displays *ngrams*.

An *ngram* is a group of consecutive words. The number of words in the group defines the ngram. For example, in the previous sentence, the 5-word ngrams are

> The number of words in
>
> number of words in the
>
> of words in the group

words in the group defines

in the group defines the

the group defines the ngram

We desire an app to read a Word manuscript perhaps composed of several Word files, and present tables of 2-, 3-, 4-, and 5-word ngrams of the text.

Why do this in Access? Surely we could do it in MSWord itself, because that's where all the words are. The reasons to choose Access are its database capabilities. These have no counterpart in MSWord.

Tables we'll need

Words
The words as we retrieve them from the files. This is raw data.

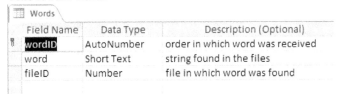

Field Name	Data Type	Description (Optional)
wordID	AutoNumber	order in which word was received
word	Short Text	string found in the files
fileID	Number	file in which word was found

Figure 26 Words Table

Files
We'd like to know what file contains specific words so we can open that file and edit the occurrence.

Files		
Field Name	Data Type	Description (Optional)
fileID	AutoNumber	shorter than a file name
fName	Short Text	file examined

Figure 27 Files table

Ones, Twos, Threes, Fours, Fives

It will take some processing to fill these tables, and we only want to do the job once per manuscript. We calculate these tables one time, and use them as sources for our queries. They all have the same shape, like this

Ones		
Field Name	Data Type	Description (Optional)
nGramID	AutoNumber	unique ID
nGram	Short Text	it
fileID	Number	source

Figure 28 Ngram tables

Relationships

The only relationships in the database we're building is between Files and the other tables.

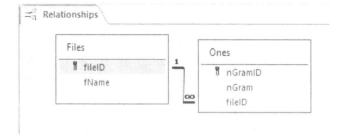

The other ngram tables have the same relationship to *Files*.

A high-level outline of the program

It helps to think through what we're going to do ahead of time, as much as possible. Even so, we'll overlook some things, and we'll have to come back and address them. Before you look at our solution, you might take a break and write down what you would do to produce this app.

1. The app has to know where the manuscript file(s) are. We'll assume they're all in a single folder. The Microsoft Office file dialog will probably be useful for getting the folder name of interest. We'll use a Form to activate it, but we'll delay building it until last.

2. The app will use the folder name to collect the file names.

3. It will open each file and extract the "words" into a table called *Words*.

4. Because Microsoft Word considers every "word" in a document to include the space following it, if it's there, and it can break punctuation marks in "funny" ways, *Words* will need some cleanup.

5. After cleaning up the words, the app will form and store the ngrams in separate tables. This will allow us to write queries to present the ngrams in helpful ways, such as counts of each.

This will conclude the development; we want to say "this is all it does". If we don't put a limit on development, we succumb to mission creep, where we are tempted to add "just one more feature". It's easy to see how this app can be extended to include Form(s) to present options to "a user". However, such extensions are unnecessary for us, as we are the users, and we have a manuscript in mind, and we know how to use a database.

Testing

It's always nice to have some data lying around that we can use for tests. We want stuff that is disposable in case we destroy it, and can be created anew in case we do destroy it. A **copy** of files of our manuscript for this book will work admirably.

We'll set up two folders:

- We'll set up a new folder in our file system called NGrams, in which we'll open our new database called *NGramsDB.accdb*.
- We'll make a subfolder called NGramsTest into which we'll insert a file or two.
- We'll use some random folder that has no Word files in it to test "the zero case" when there's nothing that can be done. Testing for this case will be in the Form.

By knowing where our files are, we can delay building a form to find them, and simply start executing code from within the app. This is an example of Commandment VII, separating a Form from a Module.

While we develop our app, we'll *hardwire* the folder names into our code. This will also save us time, because we won't have to navigate through the file system every time we want to run a test.

With this plan, we satisfy both 1. and 2. of the high-level outline.

Setting up the VBE

If we add the Word object model to our environment, it will add *Intellisense* capabilities as we write our code.

Later, when we need the Microsoft Office file dialog to find the actual files, we'll probably need a reference to the Microsoft Office Object Library, too, so we'll add that as well. Our Available References will look like this:

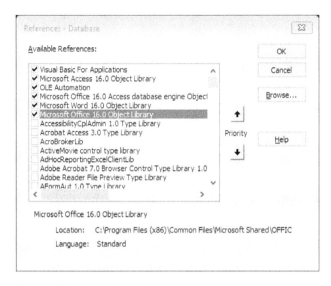

Figure 29 Available References

Writing the code

We haven't written a lick of code yet, but we have tables, relations between them, and a plan. Now we need a Module. Open the VBE and insert a Module; rename it *NGramProducer*. We'll need a place to do some exploratory coding, so insert another Module and name it *Explorations*.

Still avoiding writing any code, we'll use VCA to write 120 lines of program code for us. We specify the Name as *AAANGramProducer* and the Description as *Gather "words" into ngrams*. We prefix the name with *AAA* because we sometimes use MZTools to sort the procedures into alphabetical order, and we always want this main program at the top.

The **call tree** of our generated code looks like this

```
AAANGramProducer
        Init
        Run
        Fini
```

where AAANGramProducer is a Public Sub acting
as our main program, and the other functions are
Private Functions. We'll call these the "main"
functions.

VCA also produces *test drivers*. These are Private
Subs that allow us to independently call each of
the procedures in the call tree. They have the
same names as the main functions with a prefix
"X". They are

```
XAAANGramProducer
        XInit
        XRun
        XFini
```

Since they're Private, it will be impossible for
them to be called by another Module. We'll use
XAAANGramProducer as our test driver, and
mostly ignore the others in this particular example.

Obviously, that's a lot of code already. As we present our additions and modifications, we will
omit the tracking and trapping code *from this
presentation only*. Writing code without using the
guardrails that programming to the

commandments provides is like coding nude (not a pretty sight to imagine).

The full code of the app in all its glory is downloadable from our website.

Here's the full main Sub code we start with, along with its test driver (formatted to fit this page):

```
Public Sub AAANGramProducer()
'   Purpose: AAANGramProducer – Gather "words" into ngrams
    On Error GoTo errorExit
    Enter "AAANGramProducer" ' Tracing
    Dim result as Boolean
    '==================================
    result = Init

    If (result) Then
        result = Run
    End If

    result = Fini(result)
    '==================================
exitProcessing:
    On Error Resume Next
    Leave "AAANGramProducer"
    Exit Sub

errorExit:
    Debug.Print Err.Description
    Stop
    Resume exitprocessing
    Resume

End Sub
```

```
Private Sub XAAANGramProducer
    AAANGramProducer
End Sub
```

Listing 41 Main NGram generator program

The code is structured so that whether *Init* works (returns *True*) or not, or *Run* works (returns *True*) or not, *Fini* will always be called with *result*.

A Note On Presentation
We developed this code following all the commandments, broke a few along the way, and paid the price in debugging. But since we all "know" about the prefix code at the beginning of each procedure, and the error traps at the end, we're going to omit that code and present only the code of interest. The full code is available at the book website. Instead of what you see in Listing 41, we'll present it this way, in the book:

```
Public Sub AAANGramProducer()

    result = Init

    If (result) Then
        result = Run
    End If

    result = Fini(result)

End Sub
'
Private Sub XAAANGramProducer()
    AAANGramProducer
End Sub
```

Listing 42 Main NGram generator program (presented)

to save space. Understand that all the safeguards
are actually in place, and that we can ignore them
for the moment. As you read the code, look for the
visual patterns the constructs form.

First Test

Does the program work!? NO! It fails to compile!
The compiler can't find a reference to *Trace.* We
open the References dialog again and add our
Support.accde library to the references. We press
Alt+D, Enter to compile our program (or click De-
bug | Compile Database). Then, with our cursor in
the test driver, we press F5 in our Driver program and produce the Trace messages to the Immediate window.

```
Enter AAANGramProducer
 Enter Init
 Leave Init
 Enter Fini
Failure
 Leave Fini
Leave AAANGramProducer
```

Figure 30 First Trace of working, but failing, program

It ends with the message *Failure,* as expected.
That's because we haven't fixed *Init* to return a
True value. Note that *Run* isn't even called.

Can we open MSWord?

We'll focus on making MSWord available to the
Module by using Module-wide variables.

Module-wide variables break a Rule of Good Practice:

It is good practice to declare the names and types of variables as close to their point of use as possible.

We're breaking this rule because Module-wide variables provide simplification and convenience. Such variables are available to every procedure in the Module without having to explicitly pass the variables in argument lists. They are Private to their Module by default, so in this case, *Dim* is the same as *Private*.

The challenge they provide is remembering that they exist. They are declared so far away from where we want to use them, we can overlook them.

Make MSWord available

At the top of the Module, add the module-wide variables

```
Dim MSWord      As Word.Application
Dim pathToFiles As String
Const TESTPATH  As String = "C:\Users\...\NGrams\"
```

The Good Practice shown here is

Name CONSTANTS in caps.

Change the main program

Change the main program *signature* by adding the path name, which will eventually come from our Form.

Public Sub AAANGramProducer(pathToFiles as string)

In our Test Driver, change the call to our main program to match its signature:

```
Private Sub XAAANGramProducer()
   AAANGramProducer TESTPATH
End Sub
```

Our Form, whenever we produce it, will call our main program the same way as the test driver.

For data coming into a Module, we usually do all assignments immediately. That is, we'll do the TESTPATH assignment immediately rather than passing it to *Init*.

> *The less data passed, the better.*

But we have two variables with the same name: *pathToFiles* as the *AAANGramProducer* parameter, and *pathToFiles* as the Module-wide variable. Which is which? We *disambiguate* the assignment by using the Module name like this

```
NGramProducer.pathToFiles = pathToFiles
```

because the Module-wide variable *belongs* to the Module. We can always use the Module name to declare what belongs to it.

Change Initialization

In *Init*, add two lines

```
Private Function Init() As Boolean
    Set MSWord = New word.Application
    result = IsObject(MSWord)
End Function
```

IsObject is a VBA function that returns True if its argument is an object. If *MSWord* is made, then *Init* will return True.

Change Fini

In *Fini*, add a line to set MSWord = Nothing. The function will look like this

```
Private Function Fini(result As Boolean) As Boolean
    Set MSWord = Nothing
    Dim msg As String
    If result Then
        Debug.Print "Success"
        msg = "Success"
    Else
        Debug.Print "Failure"
        msg = "Failure"
    End If
End Function
```

which disposes of MSWord when we're done with it.

Test

Go to our test driver and step through the code with F8. We know we're starting to have a working program because *Init* returns True, allowing *Run* to run. *Run* returns False, though, so the program still fails. Let's look at *Run*.

Change Run

As an outline of needed code, consider

```
CollectWords
CleanupWords
MakeNgrams
```

This outline gives us the names of three more functions:

CollectWords will iterate over all of the files and put each word in the Words table. As we open a file, we'll extract the words, and then close the file. This is point 3 of the high-level outline.

CleanupWords will get rid of whatever nonwords are in the file, like the VBA continuation characters "_". This is point 4 of the high-level outline.

MakeNgrams can use the cleaned contents of the Words table to make ngrams.

In our usual style to make sure our code is working, we'll put these functions in an *If Then Else* construct over *result* as follows

```
Private Function Run() As Boolean
   result = CollectWords
   If result Then
      result = CleanupWords
      If result Then
         result = MakeNgrams
      End If
   End If
   Run = result
End Function
```

Our call tree takes on the three new functions as subordinates to Run, like this

```
AAANGramProducer
  Init
  Run
    CollectWords
    CleanupWords
    MakeNgrams
  Fini
```

We use VCA to generate the three functions. We begin our test at *XAAANGramProducer*. Execution eventually flows from *Run* into the empty *Collect-Words* and fails. So let's work on it first.

CollectWords

CollectWords will have three parts:

- Get each file name
- Save the file name to the Files table
- Extract the file contents and append them into the Words table

When we see the word "each" in one of our code outlines, that's an indication that there will be some kind of loop over a collection of things. This is a hint that we might rephrase "Get each file name": perhaps "Nextfile" will do, which maps easily to a function that returns a file name.

The second step of the outline looks straightforward, but it will have to return the fileID Access generates for the filename. We want to store the fileID as the foreign key to each word in Words (Cf. Figure 26 page 198). That reference is similar to the difficulty of using Module-wide variables – they're so far away, it's hard to find them.

In the third part of our outline, the word "and" appears, so we're thinking this might be a function that does two things. On the other hand, there's a rule of good practice that says

> *A function should do only one thing.*

We can get around this problem by changing our thinking to "Transfer the file contents to the Words table".

But wait! *Run* itself is doing more than one thing, and so do other functions ... they're each doing a *bunch* of things. If however, we say that *Run* is *controlling* these other functions, we split hairs as to what "one thing" is.

```
Private Function CollectWords() As Boolean
    Dim fname As String
    Dim fpath As String

    Do While NextFile(fname, fpath)

        Dim msg As String
        msg = "Reading " & fname
        StatusBar (msg)

        Dim fileID As Long
        result = SaveFileName(fname, fileID)
        If result Then
            result = TransferFileContents(fileID, fpath)
        End If

    Loop

    CollectWords = result
End Function
```

To test this function, we've commented out everything that follows the call of NextFile in the Do
While statement. NextFile looks like this

Nextfile

```
Private Function NextFile(fname As String, _
     fpath As String) As Boolean
  If Not beenHereBefore Then
    Dim seekPath As String
    seekPath = PathToFiles & "*.doc*"
    fname = Dir(seekPath)
    beenHereBefore = True
  Else
    fname = Dir()
  End If
  fpath = PathToFiles & fname
  result = Len(fname) > 0
End Function
```

NextFile insulates us from the file fetch nitty
gritty, and is independent of ngram production.
Therefore, we wrote and tested the code in our
Explorations Module. When we got it working, we
moved it into the *NGramProducer* Module.

When there are no more files in the folder of interest, Dir returns a zero-length string. We test
this with the built-in *Len* function. As long as *Len*
returns a number > 0 , there is another file to process.

When execution flows into *NextFile*, we want to
know "is this the first time we've been here?" We
need to know this because the VBA function *Dir*
requires a path as a parameter the first time it's
called, but none afterwards. We'll track the first
entry to NextFile with a Module-wide variable

beenHereBefore

So: the first time execution enters *NextFile*, *been-HereBefore* is False. Therefore,

Not beenHereBefore

is True. This allows us to generate the search path, and retrieve the "first file name" *fname* from the *Dir* function. We set *beenHereBefore* to True, so the next time we come back for a file, *Dir* is accessed properly.

Finally, as we exit, we calculate the full path to the file so we can pass that to MSWord.

This kind of logic is well suited to be in an insulating container rather than in a many-lined function. You may find yourself writing functions like NextFile from time to time to make the VBA interface more convenient, rather than winding yourself around the axle to accommodate the language.

SaveFileName

SaveFileName is our next step. We want to save the name in the Files table, and collect the ID used as the key so we can pass that to the Words table as a foreign key.

```
Private Function SaveFileName( fname As String, _
        fileID As Long ) As Boolean
   Dim rst As Recordset
   Set rst = CurrentDb.OpenRecordset("Files", _
        dbOpenDynaset )

    rst.AddNew
      rst!fname = fname
    rst.Update

    rst.MoveLast   '  most recent addition
    fileID = rst!fileID

   rst.Close
   Set rst = Nothing

   result = True
   SaveFileName = result
End Function
```

This function is almost independent, but it needs
the Files table. We can test it in a little loop that
passes strings and retrieves longs. It works.

TransferFileContents

TransferFileContents will complete the code necessary to collect words. We'll open the MSWord
file using MSWord invisibly, open Words using a
Recordset, copy the words, and dispose of all the
objects.

```
Private Function TransferFileContents( fileID As Long, _
        fpath As String) As Boolean
    Dim aDoc As word.Document
    Set aDoc = MSWord.Documents.Open(fpath, _
        ReadOnly:=True, Visible:=False)
      Debug.Print aDoc.Name

    Dim rst As Recordset
    Set rst = CurrentDb.OpenRecordset("Words", _
        dbOpenDynaset)

    Dim junk As Boolean
    Dim w As Variant
    For Each w In aDoc.Words
      rst.AddNew
        rst!word = w.Text
        rst!fileID = fileID
      rst.Update
      junk = AllowOtherProcesses
    Next w
    result = True

    rst.Close
    Set rst = Nothing

    aDoc.Close
    Set aDoc = Nothing
    TransferFileContents = result
End Function
```

The novel feature in *CollectWords* is the use of the
Variant variable *w* to control the For Each. We
test everything we have so far, and it all works.

Whatever code we add now can deal with the Words table, and we can leave the file system alone. This will simplify testing because we can start execution in *XMakeNgrams*.

Our calling tree now looks like

```
AAANGramProducer
  Init
  Run
    CollectWords
      NextFile
      SaveFileName
      TransferFileContents
    CleanupWords
    MakeNgrams
  Fini
```

CleanupWords

Peeking into the Words table, we find the words from our manuscript, but also strange things. Some of the words have a blank appended to them. There are what seem to be blank entries. There are quotation marks, parentheses, and other punctuation marks.

wordID ▾	word ▾	fileID ▾	C
411	lll	4	
412	.	4	
413	Thou|	**4**	
414	Shalt	4	
415	Use	4	
416	Tools	4	
417		4	
418	We	4	
419	have	4	

This is because a "word" in Word can include the blank that follows it. A "word" can also be punctuation. For the row at wordID = 413, the cursor is positioned after the blank. Word 417 looks like an empty string.

It seems that if we want **words**, we'll have to accept only bunches of characters that begin with a letter, and don't have a trailing blank. We also need to throw away all the non-word entities. Let's use an Update query with the *RTrim* function to get rid of the space at the end if each word.

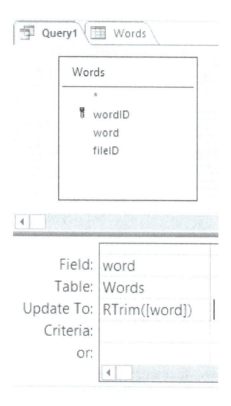

Figure 31 Query to clean data

We'll save this query as *RTrimWords*. We run the query by itself from the query design grid. It works.

Using some primeval code

We should be able to do the next step of cleanup with a query, too, although we may need a little VBA help. We want to keep only those entries in the words column that begin with a letter.

Although VBA has an *IsNumeric* function, it doesn't have an *IsAlpha* or *IsLetter* function, functions that would tell us if a string is all alphabetic characters.

VBA has the ancient function *Asc*, which returns the integer character code of the first character of a string. The help file tells us that *Asc* throws a run-time error if it gets an empty string. Great! An explicit warning that an error is possible. We want to wrap this function in one of our own, so we can Trap the error (Commandment V).

Or perhaps do something else? We don't care if the string is empty, we just want those strings that begin with a letter. So rather than *trap* an error, should one occur, we'd rather just blow by it. Also, because this function is going to be called many times, we've taken out our trace code, for real.

Here's our wrap around *Asc*

```
Public Function IsLetter (aSingleCharacter As String)_
        As Boolean
'  Purpose: IsLetter –
'      True if 1st char is a letter
' do not stop for "errors"
    On Error Resume Next
'======================================
    Dim c As Integer
    c = Asc(aSingleCharacter)
    IsLetter = (65 <= c And c <= 90) _
        Or (97 <= c And c <= 122)
'======================================
    Exit Function
End Function
```

And the test function

```
Private Sub XIsLetter()
    Dim result As Boolean
    result = IsLetter(vbNullString)
    Debug.Print "vbNullString", result
    result = IsLetter(vbCrLf)
    Debug.Print "vbCrLf", result
    result = IsLetter(".")
    Debug.Print ".", result
    result = IsLetter("A")
    Debug.Print "A", result
End Sub
```

We built this function in our *Explorations* Module, too.

Now we'd like to use it in a Select query to see
what we get,

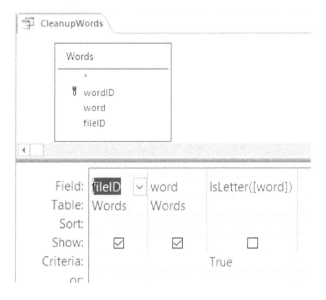

and then turn it into an Append query to extract
the words into the *Ones* table.

We want the *RTrimWords* and *CleanupWords* queries to run so that they produce clean words in
the *Ones* table. Here's how we do that in VBA, using the queries via the Access *QueryDefs* collection:

```
Private Function CleanupWords() As Boolean
    Dim qdef As QueryDef
    Set qdef = CurrentDb.QueryDefs("RTrimWords")
    qdef.Execute

    Set qdef = CurrentDb.QueryDefs("CleanupWords")
    qdef.Execute

    Set qdef = Nothing
    result = True
    CleanupWords = result
End Function
```

When this procedure runs correctly, we will have all the data we need to generate our ngrams. Since we have data in the *Words* table, we can Test this code by running it from *XCleanupWords.* Doing so fills the *Ones* table as we expect.

Clearing the tables

We ran our code more than once as we tested it, so we had to clear the tables prior to a test run. When we work with real data rather than our test stuff, we'll want clean tables then, too.

One important implication of this decision: While we're developing code, clearing data out of the tables doesn't matter. But when we go forward to our next document, or someone else's document, the 'old' data from the 'old' manuscript will be erased. Therefore, we need to warn our users that old data will be cleared out prior to the run,

and advise them to make a copy of the database if
they wish to save it.

ClearTables SQL

Access is a database, so let's use the database language: SQL. You might know how to write a query
to clear everything out of a table, but if you don't,
have Access write it for you, like this:

- Go to the Access Create menu (in the database, not the VBE).
- Click Query Design. The Show Table dialog opens. Click the Add button to add
  "Files" to the query. Close the Show Table
  dialog.
- In the Query design space, where it is
  showing the fields of the Files table, double click the asterisk. This enters "Files.*"
  in the "Field:" row, and "Files" in the "Table:" row. The "*" means "every column."
- In the Query Type panel of the Ribbon,
  click "Delete" to declare this a Delete
  query. Access adds the "Delete:" row to
  the design area, and fills it with the word
  "From".
- On your Quick Access Toolbar, click "SQL"
  to see what access wrote:

DELETE Files.*
FROM Filec;

ClearTables VBA code

Now we could write a delete query for every table in our database, but it would be easier to use VBA to assemble the SQL strings we need.

While it is true that Access table names are contained in the *TableDefs* collection, with our simple application it makes sense to make them more immediately available. Hence we declare a Module-wide array

```
Dim tableNames(1 To 7)  As String
```

and write a simple function to initialize the array

```
Private Function InitTableNames() As Boolean
    tableNames(1) = "Ones"
    tableNames(2) = "Twos"
    tableNames(3) = "Threes"
    tableNames(4) = "Fours"
    tableNames(5) = "Fives"
    tableNames(6) = "Words"
    tableNames(7) = "Files"
    result = True
    InitTableNames=result
End Function
```

A benefit of doing this initialization in a separate function is that we can call it from our test driver now, and insert a call to it in *Init* when we use the program on real data, and we don't have to rewrite it or copy and paste code.

The order of the tables in this array is also important. Because there is a Relation between Files and all the other tables, Files must be the *last* table from which deletions can be made.

Given *tableNames*, the code for *ClearTables* becomes straightforward

```
Private Function ClearTables() As Boolean
    Dim sql As String
    Dim tIndex  As Long
    For tIndex = 1 To 7
        sql = "DELETE " & tableNames(tIndex) & ".* " _
            & "FROM " & tableNames(tIndex) & ";"
        CurrentDb.Execute sql
    Next tIndex
    result = True
    ClearTables = result
End Function
```

where we use the Access *CurrentDb.Execute* method to do the work.

Testing proves it works. Now we need to call it from *Init*.

In *Init*, we insert calls to our two new functions

```
    result = InitTableNames
    result = ClearTables
```

We use this format because we've written *InitTableNames* and *ClearTables* as functions, and functions all return some value. To keep the program text clear, we call a function *as a function*, and then throw the result away.

Our call tree now looks like this

```
AAANGramProducer
 Init
  InitTableNames
  ClearTables
 Run
  CollectWords
   NextFile
   SaveFileName
   TransferFileContents
  CleanupWords
  MakeNgrams
 Fini
```

Incidentally, we are making frequent use of two capabilities of Access while we're developing code:

- The VBE Debug | Compile button. Since our VBE setup has the Auto Syntax Check turned off, we need frequent affirmation that our code is compiling. It's a good habit to have.
- The Access Compact & Repair button. This keeps the database size small, and removes cruft by making fresh copies of things. We usually use it immediately after adding a procedure.

Make the Ngrams

Tables in relational databases like Access store their rows in "random order", but we want the words in the order in which they occur in the manuscript. We *know* that the AutoNumber data type (used as a row ID) increases monotonically as rows are added to a table. This means that we can use *wordID* to determine how words are ordered in the original document.

Before we go any further, we need to look at some properties of Recordsets.

Recordsets

Normally you can't count on the order of rows in tables, because tables are *sets* which are only ordered if they're sorted. In our case, we *can* count on the order in *Ones*, because each row has a sequential ID.

If we lay out the contents of *Ones* as if it were one word after the other, it might appear like this:

III	Thou	Shalt	Use	Tools		...	

The way a Recordset sees it, it will look like this:

BOF	III	Thou	Shalt	Use	Tools		...	EOF

Figure 32 A Recordset's view of data

BOF is Beginning Of File, EOF is End Of File. It's like looking at how the table would be stored on magnetic tape, which is how databases *were* stored in the previous millennium. BOF and EOF are not data members of the table; they're just markers that will tell us where we are as we read the table.

With that in mind, let's write the code to collect ngrams.

Rather than start at a high-level view, let's look at the detail immediately. The question is: how can we make ONE ngram? If we can do that, then we can put that in a loop and make a lot of ngrams.

Let's refine the question a bit more. How can we make ONE ngram of a particular SIZE? If we can do that, then we can make many ngrams of several sizes.

Local to the procedure, we'll need

- A String in which to collect the words, call it *newNgram*
- A Long to hold the *fileID*
- A variable to count the ngrams gathered, as a looping control

From the calling procedure, we'll need

- Two Recordsets:
  - *ones*, which is derived from our cleaned up Words table
  - *newNgrams* to access the table of SIZE ngrams, into which we'll add our newly created ngram
- *ones* positioned properly

- The SIZE we're working with, so we know when to stop.

With this set of ingredients, we arrive at the code in Listing 43. As with many loops, the difficulty in writing this function is guaranteeing termination. In this case, when we detect *ones*.EOF = True, we're done. Although detection of EOF is important, what we're really after is the word count.

As we proceed towards the end-of-file, we collect and count the words that we've gathered. After each word except the last, we add a space to the ngram. For the last word, rather than adding a space, we pick up the FileID. Then we move to the next word in our Recordset.

If we hit end-of-file, the size of the ngram will be exactly the number we want, or it will be short of that desired number. Thus we need to compare those two numbers. If the number of words = ASize, we save the new ngram to the newNGrams recordset. Since we're calling a Function as if it were a Sub, we don't care if *SaveNewNgram* works or not, but we provide a place for the function return value in the variable *dontCare*. If you're not writing a book, this code should be commented appropriately so its next reader doesn't freak out.

We've used the ':' statement here to set initial values, and also to save enough vertical room to allow the code to fit on a page in this book.

> *Use the colon to initialize variables ONLY.*

Now the loop that builds the ngrams must terminate on either of two conditions:

- We've reached the end of file
- The ngram returned is not the size desired (which means there aren't enough words left in the Recordset to make an ngram of the size desired)

This is a complicated loop shut-down condition because it's probable that for some ngram size, the Recordset size is exactly divisible by the ngram size. Therefore, we've split the Do While condition to test for the ngram size as the loop terminator, and set the test for EOF condition as the criterion in an immediately following If Else. This is not an unusual circumstance, and is one of the few times we use an Exit Do to terminate an iteration.

What do you think of the variable name *dontCare*? Do you have an alternative you prefer?

.

```
Private Function MakeAnNgramOfASize( _
   ASize As Long, ones As Recordset, _
   newNgrams As Recordset) As Boolean
   Dim newNgram As String:  newNgram = vbNullString
   Dim fileID As Long
   Dim nwordsFound As Long
   Dim nsize As Long: nsize = 1
   Do While nsize <= ASize
      If ones.EOF Then  '  we're done
         Exit Do
      Else
         newNgram = newNgram & ones!ngram  '  add word
         nwordsFound = nwordsFound + 1  '  bump count
         If nsize < ASize Then        '  add a space
            newNgram = newNgram & " "
         Else  ' nsize >= ASize; pick up fileID
            fileID = ones!fileID
         End If
         ones.MoveNext
      End If
      nsize = nsize + 1
   Loop

   Dim dontCare As Boolean
   If nwordsFound = ASize Then
      dontCare = SaveNewNgram( _
         newNgrams, newNgram, fileID)
      result = True
   End If
End Function
```

Listing 43 MakeAnNgramOfASize

The *saving* task is assigned to the procedure called *SaveNewNgram* that we write like this

```
Private Function SaveNewNgram _
  ( newNgrams As Recordset _
  , newNgram As String _
  , fileID As Long _
  ) As Boolean
  newNgrams.AddNew
     newNgrams!ngram = newNgram
     newNgrams!fileID = fileID
  newNgrams.Update
  result = True
  SaveNewNgram = result
End Function
```

where I've "stacked" the arguments to the Function. This layout sometimes simplifies supplying the correct argument to a function at the correct place.

Let's look at our test driver for this procedure, as it supplies the other necessities. We'll need the *ones* and *newNgrams* Recordsets, and a size.

```
Private Sub XMakeAnNgramOfASize()
    Dim ones As Recordset
    Set ones = CurrentDb.OpenRecordset( _
            "Ones", dbOpenDynaset)
    Dim newNgrams As Recordset
    Set newNgrams = CurrentDb. OpenRecordset( _
            "Fives", dbOpenDynaset)
    Dim ASize As Long:  ASize = 5
    Dim result As Boolean
    result = MakeAnNgramOfASize(ASize, _
            ones, newNgrams)
    Debug.Print "Success = True: "; result
    newNgrams.Close
    Set newNgrams = Nothing
    ones.Close
    Set ones = Nothing
End Sub
```

For success, *MakeAnNgramOfASize* has to return
True, so we check our calculation results and set
result appropriately. Back at our test driver, we
find that 2 works, so we change the result set to
Threes and 3, Fours and 4, and Fives and 5. Everything works.

Our code gives us ONE ngram of each size; we
want them ALL, so we'll write a new function
called *MakeAllNgramsOfASize*. It'll use the same
parameters as it takes to make AN ngram, so it'll
look like this

```
Private Function MakeAllNgramsOfASize( _
    ASize As Long, _
    ones As Recordset, newNgrams As Recordset) _
    As Boolean
  Dim calcOK As Boolean:   calcOK = True
  ones.MoveFirst
  Do While calcOK
    calcOK = MakeAnNgramOfASize(ASize, _
            ones, newNgrams)
    ones.Move -(ASize - 1)
  Loop
  MakeAllNgramsOfASize = True
End Function
```

Here we're calling our Function to make An ngram, which we've already proven to work. The loop terminates when the calcOK variable becomes false. Our MakeAnNgramOfASize returns True when it has made and stored an ngram. Otherwise, it returns false, and we're done.

To acquire the next ngram, we need to reposition the *ones* Recordset: we need to move our position *back* to the next word after the one we started with. The Recordset object has several Move methods; in this case we want to go *backwards*. The Recordset object associates *backward* with a move in a negative direction, and we want to go back *aSize-1*.

Our test driver for this procedure looks familiar

```
Private Sub XMakeAllNgramsOfASize()
    Dim ones As Recordset
    Set ones = CurrentDb.OpenRecordset("Ones", _
            dbOpenDynaset)
    Dim newNgrams As Recordset
    Set newNgrams = CurrentDb.OpenRecordset("Twos", _
            dbOpenDynaset)
    Dim ASize As Long:  ASize = 2
    Dim dontCare As Boolean

    dontCare = MakeAllNgramsOfASize(ASize, ones, _
        newNgrams)

    newNgrams.Close
    Set newNgrams = Nothing
    ones.Close
    Set ones = Nothing
End Sub
```

It looks familiar because we still need the same
entities to manufacture our ngrams.

It's all working, but we notice that the *Enter-
Leave* trace is printed to the Immediate window
for every ngram. That is a flood we don't need or
want, so we've turned off that trace.

Finally, we can write *MakeAllNgramsOfAllSizes*,
or, more simply, *MakeNgrams*.

```
Private Function MakeNgrams() As Boolean
    Dim ones As Recordset
    Set ones = CurrentDb.OpenRecordset("Ones", _
        dbOpenDynaset)

    Dim newNgrams As Recordset
    Dim ASize As Long
    For ASize = 2 To 5

        Set newNgrams = CurrentDb. OpenRecordset( _
            tableNames(ASize), dbOpenDynaset)
        result = MakeAllNgramsOfASize(ASize, ones, _
            newNgrams)
        newNgrams.Close
        Set newNgrams = Nothing
    Next ASize

    ones.Close
    Set ones = Nothing
    MakeNgrams = result
End Function
```

Listing 44 MakeNGrams final

We're using *ASize* as an index into the *tableNames* array to determine the *newNgrams* Recordset.

The test driver for this procedure is simple

```
Private Sub XMakeNgrams()
    trace.Reset
    Dim result As Boolean
    result = InitTableNames
    result = MakeNgrams
End Sub
```

We use *trace.Reset* to set the trace indent back to
zero, because we've been through these procedures a few times during their development. The
other two procedure calls are familiar from our
earlier work.

Hint: When a bunch of loops gets going in Windows, it may look like a runaway. We can use the
Task Manager to End the Task, but you have to
start the Task Manager before you start your
loop.

If you stop a program via the Task Manager, you'll
probably lose some code if you haven't saved it,
so saving before executing is yet another good
practice.

Our call tree now looks like this

```
AAANGramProducer
 Init
  ClearTables
 Run
  CollectWords
   NextFile
   SaveFileName
   TransferFileContents
  CleanupWords
   IsLetter
  MakeNgrams
   MakeAllNgramsOfASize
    MakeAnNgramOfASize
     SaveNewNgram
 Fini
```

We run the app from *XMakeNgrams* and find that we have some real live ngrams of all sizes, producing elation in the programmer, and a deserved exclamation mark to end this sentence!

The Form

Go to Access (not the VBE) click on Create | Blank Form. Switch to Design View if you're not already there. Display the Property Sheet.

From the Design tab, drag a titling label, an instructions label, three buttons, and three text boxes. After changing the control names and

aligning things, it looks like this

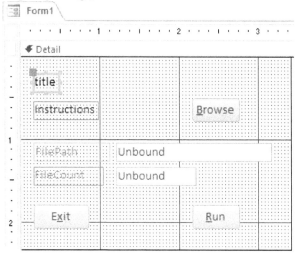

which will obviously change ere we're done.

Buttons

While we go through the button control wizards, we don't care what kind of button we're adding, so we choose Record Navigation from the Categories and Find Next from the Actions. As we click through the Command Button Wizard, we select Text for the display rather than icons, and type in E&xit so that "Alt-x" will be the accelerator for the Exit button. Similarly for the &Browse and &Run buttons.

The next wizard window asks for the name of the button. We chose "ExitButton". You can put spaces in the name, but don't.

Textboxes

The TextBoxes will contain the FilePath and FileCount, respectively. We want those to be displayed to give our user a sense that our program understands what she wants to do. However, we don't want the user to change the values in them; they're merely for display, so we'll set Enabled to No.

Title and Instructions Labels

We'll fill them in later.

That's it. The buttons are ready in the user interface. Now we need the VBA code to make them work.

VBA

Still in Access, make sure Form is selected in the Property Sheet.

1. Select the Other tab. Near the bottom of the properties, set Has Module to "Yes".
2. In the ribbon, make sure the Form Design Tools are displayed, and that the Design Tab is selected.
3. On the Property Sheet, make sure "Form" is selected in the dropdown.
4. On the Ribbon (at the far right), click "Convert Form's Macros to Visual Basic". When the Convert form pops up, click "Convert". Success is indicated by a "Conversion Finished" messagebox.

5. Save the Form! Up until now, it is only stored in memory. If you don't save it now, you may lose it!

Open the VBE.

Because the Event Subs belong to a Form, the Form itself has to be active in order to trace the execution through the Form code. Activating the Form requires some button clicking, which we want to avoid. So add another Module entitled *Form1Calc*. We'll put code here that we can test independently of the Forms.

While we've been playing with our Form, Access has loaded the *acwzmain* and *acwztool* projects to enable the wizards. You may safely ignore them. You can open them in the Project window to see the Modules that are inside them, but you can't access them unless you have the password. The projects will go away when Form design is done.

In the Project pane, under Microsoft Access Class Objects, there is our Form.

Opening it, we find the code Access wrote to respond to the button Events.

ExitButton code

The Access-written code for the Exit button looks like this

```
'--------------------------------------
' ExitButton_Click
'
'--------------------------------------
Private Sub ExitButton_Click()
On Error GoTo ExitButton_Click_Err

    DoCmd.FindNext


ExitButton_Click_Exit:
    Exit Sub

ExitButton_Click_Err:
    MsgBox Error$
    Resume ExitButton_Click_Exit

End Sub
```

Lots of space, and a useless comment telling us the name of the Sub that follows. Error$ is an alternate form of the Error function. It returns "a special value", per the help file.

Put the cursor to the immediate left of the period in the DoCmd line, like this

DoCmd|.FindNext

and type another period, so it looks like this

Intellisense opens a dropdown that shows all the legitimate text that can now be added. Scroll down the list to "Quit", and select it (or simply type it in). The VBE now looks like this

DoCmd.Quit|.FindNext

Select to the end of the line and delete ".Find-Next", so we're left with

DoCmd.Quit

Save and compile. Save everything, because we're going to test the Quit button.

Do a File Compact and Repair, and close Access.

Open Access again, and double click the Form to open it. Click the Quit button. Everything closes. Good. It works.

This is one of those cases when you don't need much other than the DoCmd statement so we throw everything extraneous away.

```
Private Sub ExitButton_Click()
    DoCmd.Quit
End Sub
```

BrowseButton code

In this case, we gut the Sub Access wrote for us and provide our own outline for the code:

```
Private Sub BrowseButton_Click()
'    use msoFileDialogFolderPicker
'    if theres a selection then
'        vet the path
'        announce the selected folder
'        count files
'        announce file count
'    end if
End Sub
```

Using the *FileDialog* is supposedly simple. Our preference would be that in selecting a folder, the contents of the folder would be visible to the user. They're not, but we presume that anyone who has been working with a document knows the contents of the folder of interest. Our preference is to use Windows Explorer to find a more complete display of folders, and copy the folder name from there into the folder picker dialog. Help doesn't give a lot of detail about finding Folders. After poking around Help and the internet, we arrive at

```
Dim result As Boolean
Dim fd As Office.FileDialog
Set fd =Application.FileDialog(msoFileDialogFolderPicker)
fd.Title = "Select a Folder"
result = fd.Show
```

If *fd.Show* returns False, nothing was selected. Because we want path and *fileCount* available across the Module, we declare them as Module-wide, and we won't have to access the TextBoxes to get their values. Thus we write

```
If result Then
    path = fd.SelectedItems(1)
    path = VetPath(path)
    fileCount = CountFiles(path)
    result = FillTextBoxes(path, fileCount)
End If
Set fd = Nothing
result = BrowseSuccess(fileCount)
```

This shows us that we need four more functions: *VetPath*, *CountFiles*, *FillTextBoxes*, and *BrowseSuccess*.

If we wrote all of these in *Form_Form1*, we'd need to actually click the Browse button to check each of them, so we put them in *Form1Calc*. There, we can test them individually and independently. We can also simplify BrowseButton_Click to the following

```
Private Sub BrowseButton_Click()
'
   On Error GoTo BrowseButton_Click_Err
   ClearTextBoxes
   RunButton.Enabled = False

   Dim result As Boolean

   result = GetPathAndMSWordFileCount (path, fileCount)
   If result Then
     result = FillTextBoxes (path, fileCount)
     RunButton.Enabled = BrowseSuccess(fileCount)
   End If

BrowseButton_Click_Exit:
   Exit Sub

BrowseButton_Click_Err:
   MsgBox Error$
   Resume BrowseButton_Click_Exit

End Sub
```

where we've pulled the guts that do independent calculations into yet another independent function *GetPathAndMSWordFileCount*. It will deal with the Microsoft Office FileDialog on its own, like this

```
Public Function GetPathAndMSWordFileCount( _
    path As String, fileCount As Long) As Boolean
  Dim fd As Office.FileDialog
  Dim result as Boolean
  Set fd = Application.FileDialog _
           (msoFileDialogFolderPicker)
  fd.Title = "Select a Folder"
  result = fd.Show
  If result Then
    path = fd.SelectedItems(1)
    path = VetPath(path)
    fileCount= CountMSWordFiles(path)
  End If
  Set fd = Nothing
    GetPathAndMSWordFileCount = result
End Function
```

Which shows whence *VetPath* and *CountMSWord-Files* are called,

VetPath code

```
Public Function VetPath (path As String) As String
  VetPath = path
  If Right(VetPath, 1) <> "\" Then
    VetPath = VetPath & "\"
  End If
End Function
```

The Microsoft Office FileDialog returns folder names, but they lack the trailing "\" that allows us to easily add a filename and get a full path to a file. Hence, we check the rightmost character and add the backslash, if necessary.

The call to *VetPath* may look "unconventional", in which *path* is sent to the function as a parameter and is returned corrected as the function's value. When we write the call this way. It shows that the path parameter might change when this function is called. Cf. the call to *Fini*.

CountMSWordFiles code

We're back to our old friend, the *Dir* function. *CountMSWordFiles* is similar to the code we used in *NextFile*; this time we're simply doing a count. If there are no files in the Browsed folder, it's no use doing any further processing.

```
Public Function CountMSWordFiles (path As String) As Long
    Dim fname As String
    Dim result as Long
    Const EXT As String = "*.doc*"
    fname = Dir(path & EXT)
    Do While Len(fname) > 0
      result = result + 1
      fname = Dir()
    Loop
    CountMSWordFiles = result
End Function
```

FillTextBoxes code

FillTextBoxes sets the focus on each of the text-boxes in turn and fills them with the proper information. Because this task requires that the text-boxes have the focus ere their properties are accessed, this code belongs in *Form_Form1*. It's return value is irrelevant.

```
Private Function FillTextBoxes (path As String, _
    fileCount As Long) As Boolean
  Dim result as Boolean
  Me.TextFilePath.SetFocus
  Me.TextFilePath.Text = path
  Me.TextFileCount.SetFocus
  Me.TextFileCount.Text = fileCount
  result = True
  FillTextBoxes = result
End Function
```

BrowseSuccess code

This function either allows us to proceed, or issues an error message.

```
Private Function BrowseSuccess (fileCount As Long) _
    As Boolean
  Dim result as Boolean
  If fileCount > 0 Then
    result = True
  Else
    Dim msg As String
    msg = "NO MSWord files in this folder." & vbCrLf
    msg = msg & "Please select another."
    MsgBox msg, vbOKOnly, "NO FILES"
  End If
  BrowseSuccess = result
End Function
```

We ignore the value MsgBox returns, a little
sloppy...

RunButton code

This is now quite a simple function, most of it written by Access. We plug in the appropriate modifications, and the Form development is pretty much done.

```
Private Sub RunButton_Click()
'
    On Error GoTo RunButton_Click_Err

    AAANGramProducer path

RunButton_Click_Exit:
    Exit Sub

RunButton_Click_Err:
    MsgBox Error$
    Resume RunButton_Click_Exit

End Sub
```

A few things remain to be addressed, though.

In Real Life

Even with all our safeguards, stuff happens. In real life, things go bump in the night, and also in the day.

Data Destruction

When we first wrote *CleanupWords*, we hastily wrote this query

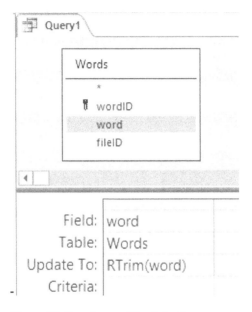

Figure 33 Cleaning up Words by Query

Before you read further: can you spot the error?

Access changes the query to this

Figure 34 What Access does with the query

This change is a disaster for us! It turns every entry in the word field into the String "word". All our data, *gone!* Ouch! I'm glad I chose disposable test data.

This semi-calamity happens because Access makes a guess. *I* as the human can see 'word' is a field. The *VBA compiler* sees *RTrim*, whose argument is a String. It stops looking for anything else. The VBE knows a String is represented by characters surrounded by double quotes, so to "help" us, it supplies them around *word*, since we "left them out".

The correct way to show that we want a *field* is to enclose it in [brackets]. Be Explicit! extends to the whole database and to the authors of books.

Files gone missing

When we tried to open a document with MSWord, the test result was a message caught by our error fumbler:

> *"Sorry, we couldn't find your file. Was it moved, renamed, or deleted?"*

followed by the default path to our Word Documents folder. We went back to the Word documentation of the call to *Documents.Open.* We read a bit more of the text and discovered that the *filename* is required, it is a *Variant*, and that

> *"The name of the document (paths are accepted)".*

Paths are not only *accepted*, they're **REQUIRED**.

Which means, Testing works, and in this case, immediately informed us of a problem. That's what we want! Best get notified now than a few months from now from one of our users! Cf. Commandment IV.

It also means that we were fortunate to choose as a test folder one other than the default Word documents folder. Had we done that, we might've missed this error.

And it also means that we can't always interpret test results correctly, even when we think we know what we want.

Files that match the filename pattern but are bogus

MSWord will try its best to open an input file looking for words. If it can't find words, it gives up with an error whose message is that the file seems to be corrupt. That's good. To deal with this error, we comment out the *Stop* statement in *TransferFileContents*, essentially eating the error.

Assuming too much

When we wrote *IsLetter* the first time, we wrote the main line of the function as

```
result = 65 <= c And c <= 122
```

because we assumed that since "A" was character 65 and "z" was character 122, that the character set was continuous. Nope! A quick check like 122 – 65 = 57 would've shown us that there's more characters than 2 x 26. The set includes the characters "[\]^_`" between "Z" and "a", so to test for letters only, the main line of the Function has to exclude those characters using this statement instead result = (65 <= c And c <= 90) Or (97 <= c And c <= 122)

Assuming too little

When we set up the database, we specified the ngram field size to be 50. With some of the long words in our test file, we exceeded that limit with several 5-grams. So we changed all the field sizes to 255, which is too large. However, Access manages the storage for strings up to the limit specified. It'll cost us a little in execution speed, but so what.

Timing the calculation

Opening the input files and gathering the words seems to take the most time in our test runs. With more input files, everything else on the computer will be halted until our program runs. It will probably be beneficial to

- Allow other processes to work while we're chugging in the background, and
- Show that the program is working.

Allow other processes

If we give other programs a bit of time during our calculation, we can do things unrelated to the ngram calculation, should we so choose. VBA supports this idea with the *DoEvents* function. We'll tuck calls to this Function in our own Function *AllowOtherProcesses* as follows

```
Private Function AllowOtherProcesses() As Boolean
  On Error Resume Next

  Static callCount As Long
  If callCount > 2147483000 Then
    callCount = 0
  End If
  callCount = callCount + 1
  If callCount Mod 500 = 0 Then
    DoEvents
  End If

End Function
```

Because we'll be calling this function a few thousand times, we've removed the tracing, and we'll eat all errors.

Note that *callCount* is declared as Static. This means that the value doesn't change between calls to this function. We don't really care what its value is, just that it is continuous, and that we don't make it larger than the largest Long value.

Show the program is working

Well-designed programs, in addition to allowing other programs to run, show that "there is something going on" by displaying an hourglass (in the old days), or the spinning toilet bowl (these days). We can do the same. The easiest way to do it is to wrap the code in our main Sub with calls like this

```
DoCmd.Hourglass True
   ...long running code
DoCmd.Hourglass False
```

It's important that we get to the line of code that
turns the Hourglass off. Our code should do that.

At the same time, it's helpful to have an idea of
what's going on in a bit more detail. In a similar
manner to our *Enter / Leave* code, it would be
useful to announce what our program is doing by
posting messages somewhere.

We might post them on the calling Form. This requires the Form be passed to our Module. The
easiest way to do that is through the argument
list of our main program, like this

```
Public Sub AAANGramProducer( PathToFiles As String, _
   callingForm As Form)
```

adding a Module-wide variable

```
Dim theForm    As Form
```

and then setting theForm like this

```
Set theForm = callingForm
```

in our main program. The code to call our Module
will have to change to

```
AAANGramProducer path, Me
```

where "Me" is the short-hand way to refer to a Form in its Module.

But this seems like too much work. Therefore, we opt to post messages to the Access Statusbar. Checking the internet, we find this code at mead-inkent.co.uk/astatus.htm:

```
Private Sub StatusBar( Optional msg As Variant)
'   lasciate ogni speranza voi ch'entrate
    Dim junk As Variant
    If Not IsMissing(msg) Then
      If msg <> "" Then
        junk = SysCmd(acSysCmdSetStatus, msg)
      Else
        junk = SysCmd(acSysCmdClearStatus)
      End If
    Else
      junk = SysCmd(acSysCmdClearStatus)
    End If
End Sub
```

Several tests of this, and reorganized versions, shows that this is sensitive code. We got it to *not* work in several configurations, so we've left it pretty much alone, and tender our thanks to Mead in Kent.

We'll use it to post the names of files as they're read, along with the progress we make with forming the ngrams.

Final Adjustments

We make the corrections to Form1 as follows

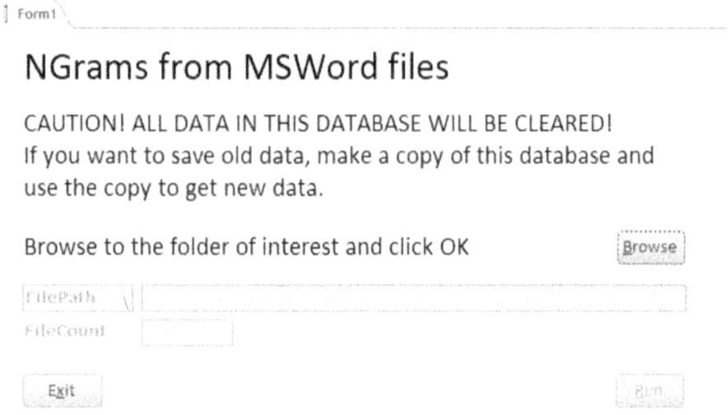

NGrams from MSWord files

CAUTION! ALL DATA IN THIS DATABASE WILL BE CLEARED!
If you want to save old data, make a copy of this database and
use the copy to get new data.

Browse to the folder of interest and click OK   Browse

FilePath
FileCount

Exit   Run

Figure 35 Final Main Form

This is one place where you can spend a lot of time tweaking things.

Then, we go to the Files | Options dialog (Figure 36) and set the Display Form to Form1, and click OK. Save the file one last time, exit out of Access. The next time the database is opened, Form1 is open and ready to go.

Make a copy of the file in a safe place, and make sure it's tracked by your backup software.

Access Options

General	
Current Database	Options for the current database.
Datasheet	
Object Designers	**Application Options**
Proofing	Application Title: NGramsDB
Language	Application Icon:
Client Settings	☐ Use as Form and Report Icon
	Display Form: Form1 ▼
	Web Display Form: (none) ▼

Figure 36 Access Options setting Form

Bibliography

We've found the following books helpful at various times of our programming life. Of most use lately are the timeless texts by Getz et. al., because they have lots of solid, tested code examples. Listed here alphabetically.

A Discipline of Programming by Edsger W. Dijkstra, ISBN-13: 978-0132158718

Access Cookbook, 2nd Edition, by Ken Getz, Paul Litwin, Andy Baron, ISBN-13: 978-0596006785

Access Solutions: Tips, Tricks, and Secrets from Microsoft Access MVPs by Arvin Meyer, Douglas J. Steele, ISBN-13: 978-0470591680

Algorithms + Data Structures = Programs, by Niklaus Wirth, ISBN-13: 978-0130224187

Developing Time-Oriented Database Applications in SQL, by Richard T. Snodgrass, ISBN-13: 978-1558604360

Joe Celko's SQL for Smarties: Advanced SQL Programming, by Joe Celko, ISBN-13: 978-0128007617

Joe Celko's SQL Programming Style, by Joe Celko, ISBN-13: 978-0120887972

Joe Celko's Thinking in Sets: Auxiliary, Temporal, and Virtual Tables in SQL, by Joe Celko, ISBN-13: 978-0123741370

Microsoft Access 2010 Inside Out, by Jeff Conrad & John L. Viescas, ISBN-13: 978-8120344594

Microsoft Access 2010 Programmer's Reference, by Teresa Hennig, ISBN-13: 978-8126528127

Microsoft Access 2010 VBA Programming Inside Out by Andrew Couch (1-Aug-2011) ISBN-13: 978-8120344594

Microsoft Office Access 2007 VBA 1st Edition, by Scott D. Diamond, Brent Spaulding ISBN-13: 978-0789737311

Pascal User Manual and Report: ISO Pascal
Standard 4th Edition by Kathleen Jensen, Niklaus
Wirth, A.B. Mickel, J.F. Miner, ISBN-13: 978-
0387976495

Software Tools 1st Edition, by Brian W. Ker-
nighan, P. J. Plauger, ISBN-13: 978-
0201036695

About the Author

Peter N Roth, MSE, has decades of experience programming, teaching and mentoring engineers, and has used, misused, abused, and been abused by, a wide variety of languages, operating systems, and programs on myriad computing platforms, and is still standing. He gained most of his experience building mainframe software to model the physical responses of underwater structures to unusual loading situations. He has been a top 5% contributor to the Microsoft Access Developers Forum.

Pete is the president of Engineering Objects International. The company focuses on database design and implementation, software tools, and software training.

You can contact him through his website https://vbafornewbies.com

INDEX

INDEX